UCHICAGO Consortium on School Research

RESEARCH REPORT   MAY 2020

The Forgotten Year

Applying Lessons from Freshman Sucess to Sophomore Year

Alex Seeskin, Shelby Mahaffie, and Alexandra Usher

TABLE OF CONTENTS

ACKNOWLEDGEMENTS

The authors gratefully acknowledge the many people who contributed to this report. To&Through Project team members Jasmin Lee, Dominique McKoy, Jenny Nagaoka, and Paulina Torres-Orejuela all provided valuable support and feedback throughout the analysis and writing process. Jessica Tansey was an essential thought-partner throughout the writing process. Sara Kempner and Consortium Steering Committee members Greg Jones and Pranav Kothari offered very thoughtful reviews as we finalized the narrative. We thank members of the UChicago Consortium's research review group, particularly John Easton, as well as Elaine Allensworth and Alyssa Blanchard. Throughout the process, we received essential feedback from the Network for College Success, particularly from Eliza Moeller, Que Keith, Lakisha Pittman, and the NCS Data Collaborative. The UChicago Consortium's communications team, including Lisa Sall, Jessica Puller, and Alida Mitau, and the UEI communication team of Dayna Dion and May Malone, were instrumental in the production of this report and its accompanying materials. Several people from Chicago Public Schools gave us feedback at various stages in the report process, and we are grateful to Jeff Broom, Molly Burke, Sarah Dickson, Amanda Hormanski, and the team from Chicago Academy for their partnership in providing context and feedback on implications. We also want to thank CPS for sharing the data that made this report possible.

This report was supported by the Crown Family Philanthropies and Crankstart. We thank them for their support and collaboration on the To&Through Project.

The UChicago Consortium gratefully acknowledges the Spencer Foundation and the Lewis-Sebring Family Foundation, whose operating grants support the work of the UChicago Consortium, and also appreciates the support from the Consortium Investor Council that funds critical work beyond the initial research: putting the research to work, refreshing the data archive, seeding new studies, and replicating previous studies. Members include: Brinson Foundation, CME Group Foundation, Crown Family Philanthropies, Lloyd A. Fry Foundation, Joyce Foundation, Lewis-Sebring Family Foundation, McDougal Family Foundation, Polk Bros. Foundation, Robert McCormick Foundation, Spencer Foundation, Steans Family Foundation, Square One Foundation, and The Chicago Public Education Fund.

Cite as: Seeskin, A., Mahaffie, S., & Usher, A. (2020). *The forgotten year: Applying lessons from Freshman success to Sophomore year.* Chicago, IL: University of Chicago Consortium on School Research.

This report was produced by the UChicago Consortium's publications and communications staff: Lisa Sall, Director of Outreach and Communication; Jessica Tansey, Communications Manager; Jessica Puller, Communications Specialist; and Alida Mitau, Development and Communications Coordinator.

Graphic Design: Jeff Hall Design
Photography: Eileen Ryan
Editing: Jessica Tansey and Jessica Puller

05.2020/PDF/jh.design@rcn.com

Executive Summary

For many students, sophomore year can be a forgotten year, a time sandwiched between high school's more momentous milestones. As a result, sophomore year lacks a clear identity, but is also well-positioned to be a time of intentional development for high school students. The purpose of this report is to help build an organizing purpose for sophomore year by developing a research-based organizing set of indicators for sophomore educators.

Using Freshman OnTrack and more nuanced definitions of freshman success, sophomore educators can better target intervention and support from the beginning of sophomore year; and using similar sophomore success indicators, they can monitor and support students during sophomore year. This report has several key findings:

Key Findings

1. **Sophomore year presents educators with an additional opportunity to identify and intervene with students who need more support.** At the beginning of sophomore year, with some relatively simple indicators—freshman off-track status, course failures, and low attendance—sophomore educators can identify most of the students who are unlikely to graduate without additional intervention. By the end of sophomore year, the predicitivy of similar indicators—sophomore off-track status, course failures, and low attendance—becomes even stronger. By layering on GPA, educators can further identify students who need additional support to gain access to selective post-secondary opportunities.

2. **For students who were off-track during freshman year, sophomore year can be an opportunity to recover. For some students who were on-track during freshman year, especially those with any Fs or low attendance, sophomore year can be a time of significant risk.** There is often meaningful movement in students' on-track status, course performance, and attendance from freshman to sophomore year of high school, and this movement can have significant implications for students' eventual outcomes.

3. **Freshman year remains the most critical year in students' educational trajectories, and even with rising Freshman OnTrack rates, the Freshman OnTrack metric remains predictive of high school graduation.** The findings from this report confirm previous conclusions from the University of Chicago Consortium on School Research (UChicago Consortium) and others about the importance of freshman year. Nearly 50 percent of the non-graduates from the 2014–15 freshman cohort were off-track during freshman year, and another 20 percent showed an additional warning indicator—a course failure or low attendance—during their freshman year.

4. **Educators can monitor more subtle warning indicators, including all course failures and low attendance, to provide support to a wider group of students in need.** In addition to Freshman OnTrack and Sophomore OnTrack indicators, schools can use more nuanced indicators to identify students who are likely to need further support in order to be successful.

5. **Freshmen and sophomores with reasonably strong grades but low attendance are in danger of not graduating without additional monitoring and support.** Students' freshman and sophomore attendance can provide insight into their likelihood of graduating from high school, independent of their freshman grades and course failures. Students from the 2014–15 freshman cohort with attendance below 85 percent during their freshman year were just as likely to not graduate as students who were off-track, and even students who passed their freshman courses with high grades were in danger of not graduating from high school if they missed three or more days of school per month.

Introduction

In Chicago and many districts around the country, sophomore year can be a forgotten year. It is a time sandwiched between high school's more momentous milestones: freshman year is focused on ensuring a smooth transition to high school, junior year on preparing for post-secondary entrance exams, and senior year on planning for a post-secondary pathway. However, the lack of definition around sophomore year is neither predetermined nor purposeful.

Without the pressures of integrating into or out of a school community, sophomore year could be a time of intentional development for students; a time to focus on the rigor of relevant coursework and to imagine a future of post-secondary possibility and adulthood.

In Chicago, high school principals and sophomore educators (by which we mean practitioners inside of schools who work directly with sophomores) can draw lessons from the district's work over the past 15 years around freshman year and Freshman OnTrack. With the adoption of Freshman OnTrack more than a decade ago—a research-based indicator that tied freshman grades and credits to students' likelihood of graduating from high school—freshman educators gained a clear organizing purpose. They were able to use Freshman OnTrack to build and improve systems to monitor and support students during their transition to high school.

However, despite the abundance of research on freshman year and the use of Freshman OnTrack in Chicago Public Schools (CPS) and other districts, we know relatively little about the parallels for sophomore year, and have not yet explored the relationship between students' Freshman OnTrack status and their Sophomore OnTrack status (a metric developed and currently monitored by CPS), how many students fall off-track for the first time during their sophomore year, or whether other indicators during sophomore year might predict graduation or college enrollment. The absence of a research-based early-warning indicator system makes it difficult for sophomore educators to reliably target supports and interventions to their students at the beginning of, and during, sophomore year.

This study seeks to develop a research-based set of indicators for sophomore year, building from the lessons of the district's work around Freshman OnTrack. We also expand our focus beyond high school graduation to include the more ambitious goals of college and career readiness. To do so, we address five research questions:

1. As Freshman OnTrack rates have improved, how, if at all, has the predictive power of Freshman OnTrack changed?

2. How accurately does Sophomore OnTrack predict high school graduation? What is the relationship between students' freshman and sophomore year performance?

3. What indicators can sophomore educators use at the beginning of sophomore year to understand the needs of their incoming students?

4. What indicators can sophomore educators use during sophomore year to monitor students' progress toward high school graduation and post-secondary success?

5. How frequently do students change success categories from freshman to sophomore year of high school, and what are the high school and college outcomes of students in different success categories?

In **Chapter 1**, we review the existing research and practice around Freshman OnTrack in order to understand how the indicator has been used in Chicago and to what extent it still predicts high school graduation. In **Chapter 2**, we review how CPS has defined Sophomore OnTrack, look at the trends over time, and consider the relationship between Freshman OnTrack and Sophomore OnTrack. In **Chapters 3 and 4**, we propose a more nuanced set of Freshman Success Categories and Sophomore Success Categories that use a system of indicators to allow educators to better monitor students' progress. Finally, in **Chapter 5**, we look closely at different groups of students' freshman and sophomore success, and their respective pathways to high school graduation and college enrollment.

On their own, indicators can't and won't change a system, but our hope is that this research, combined with these new indicators, will draw attention to the importance of sophomore year. Many schools have already built effective systems using Freshman OnTrack data. We now have the opportunity to transfer and extend that knowledge about how to monitor and support students to sophomore year so that more students graduate and have the best chance at post-secondary success.

CHAPTER 1

Freshman OnTrack in Chicago Public Schools

Freshman OnTrack

At the end of freshman year, a CPS student is considered on-track for high school graduation if:

1 They have no more than **1 core course* failure** in ninth grade

&

5 And have **earned 5 credits**, enough to be promoted to tenth grade

_____

Note: *English, math, science, social studies

Although this report focuses on research and tools for sophomore educators, it builds upon the successes of Freshman OnTrack work at CPS. A brief history of Freshman OnTrack, including lessons learned, can serve as a foundation for the development of a set of freshman and sophomore indicator categories for use by sophomore educators.

Over the past decade, CPS high schools have relied on Freshman OnTrack as a key indicator to track and understand freshman students' progress toward high school graduation.[1] Freshman OnTrack rates have been on an upward trend since 1998, but it was after schools began receiving more regular Freshman OnTrack data from the district in 2008 that the growth in the Freshman OnTrack rate accelerated (**see Figure B.1 in Appendix B**).[2] The graduation rate has also grown for the same freshman cohorts of students: since 2006, the graduation rate has grown for students of all races and genders (**see Appendix B**).

Notably, while the work to support freshmen across the district has become increasingly sophisticated and widespread, the Freshman OnTrack indicator remains consistently predictive of high school outcomes.

Yet in every cohort, there have been students who were on-track as freshmen, but did not graduate; likewise, there have been students who were off-track as freshmen, but did go on to graduate from high school within four years. This does not mean that the Freshman OnTrack indicator has become less predictive; just that it is not, and has never been, a perfect indicator. In fact, an indicator that perfectly predicted whether students would graduate based on their performance freshman year would mean that their destiny was fixed and that no amount of effort during high school could change their course. The fact that some students who were off-track as freshmen do graduate suggests that proper supports and interventions can and do change outcomes for students: with the right support, students who struggled during freshman year were able to recover and graduate from high school.

Although Freshman OnTrack remains a critical tool for freshman educators, it is not enough. On-track students who failed one course may be behind in credit accumulation and need to take the time to make up that course. Others may be passing all their courses but earning very low grades or struggling with attendance. Students who just cross the threshold of the on-track definition at the end of freshman year are still in danger of falling off-track

---

1 While the UChicago Consortium often uses the terms "ninth grade" and "tenth grade," we purposefully chose to use the terms "freshman" and "sophomore" for this report. See Data Definitions on p.33 in Appendix A for more details.

2 Roderick, Kelley-Kemple, Johnson, & Beechum (2014).

Indicators that Support Freshman OnTrack Work at CPS

Over the past decade, the Freshman OnTrack indicator has empowered CPS high schools to target supports and interventions to the students who could most benefit from them. The Freshman OnTrack indicator is grounded in previous Consortium research, which demonstrates that students' freshman course failures are highly predictive of whether or not they will graduate from high school.[A] It defines a student to be on-track if they fail no more than one semester of a core course and accumulate at least five credits by the end of their freshman year. Whether a student is on-track or off-track at the end of their freshman year is highly predictive of whether they will graduate from high school.[B]

CPS administrators added Freshman OnTrack to the district's school accountability system in 2003, but paired the accountability with a relatively high degree of autonomy and largely shied away from district mandates as to how schools should organize their freshman success work. The district has championed the importance of Freshman OnTrack and related indicators, encouraged the sharing of strategies and best practices across schools, and provided schools with timely and actionable data to inform the work. Within high schools, Freshman OnTrack work looks different in every building, but has generally been executed through a team structure, with school staff coming together to analyze Freshman OnTrack data and discuss interventions or strategies for individuals or groups of students.[C]

More recently, high schools have begun to incorporate additional research-based indicators in their work with freshmen. A 2014 Consortium study found that many students in danger of struggling during the critical transition to high school can be identified before they enter freshman year, using their eighth-grade attendance and grades.[D] Based on this research, many schools have begun looking at students' eighth-grade GPA and attendance at the beginning of their freshman year, in order to gain a more robust understanding of the needs of their incoming students. The district has also begun to highlight a freshman GPA of 3.0 or higher as an important indicator to monitor in addition to Freshman OnTrack. This work draws from previous Consortium research about the general importance of GPA,[E] and from research demonstrating that freshman grades predict a range of important outcomes, including high school graduation, college enrollment, and college persistence.[F]

Many freshman teams use these indicators in tandem to support students throughout their freshman year: they use eighth-grade attendance and grades data to better understand their incoming freshman class, and then continue to monitor students' Freshman OnTrack status and GPA throughout the school year, responding to changes in students' performance that might indicate a need for further support or intervention.

A   Allensworth & Easton (2005); Allensworth & Easton (2007).
B   Allensworth & Easton (2005).
C   Phillips (2019).
D   Allensworth, Gwynne, Moore, & de la Torre (2014).

E   Allensworth, Healy, Gwynne, & Crespin (2016); Allensworth & Clark (2018); Roderick et al. (2006).
F   Easton, Johnson, & Sartain (2017).

---

during sophomore year without additional support.

Although on-track rates have improved over time, the percentage of on-track freshmen and off-track freshmen who graduate from high school has stayed virtually unchanged (**see Figure 1**). In other words, although more students are now on-track, a student's on-track status remains a strong indicator of whether they will graduate from high school. For sophomore educators, this means that focusing on off-track freshmen can be an effective way to identify students who need extra support at the beginning of sophomore year.

As CPS high schools have become more successful at Freshman OnTrack work, fewer students are off-track

as freshmen and more students are graduating every year. The number of non-graduates from each cohort has fallen, but a larger proportion of the remaining non-graduates were on-track as freshmen (**see Figure 2**). This suggests an opportunity to shift some of the focus to some of the students who are on-track at the end of freshman year but may require supports or interventions during sophomore in order to graduate from high school. In this report, we will explore additional indicators that can help sophomore educators better identify students who may need that support. However, it is first necessary to better understand the existing Sophomore OnTrack indicator.

FIGURE 1

The Predictiveness of Freshman OnTrack Has Held Over Time

Graduation rate of on-track and off-track freshmen over time

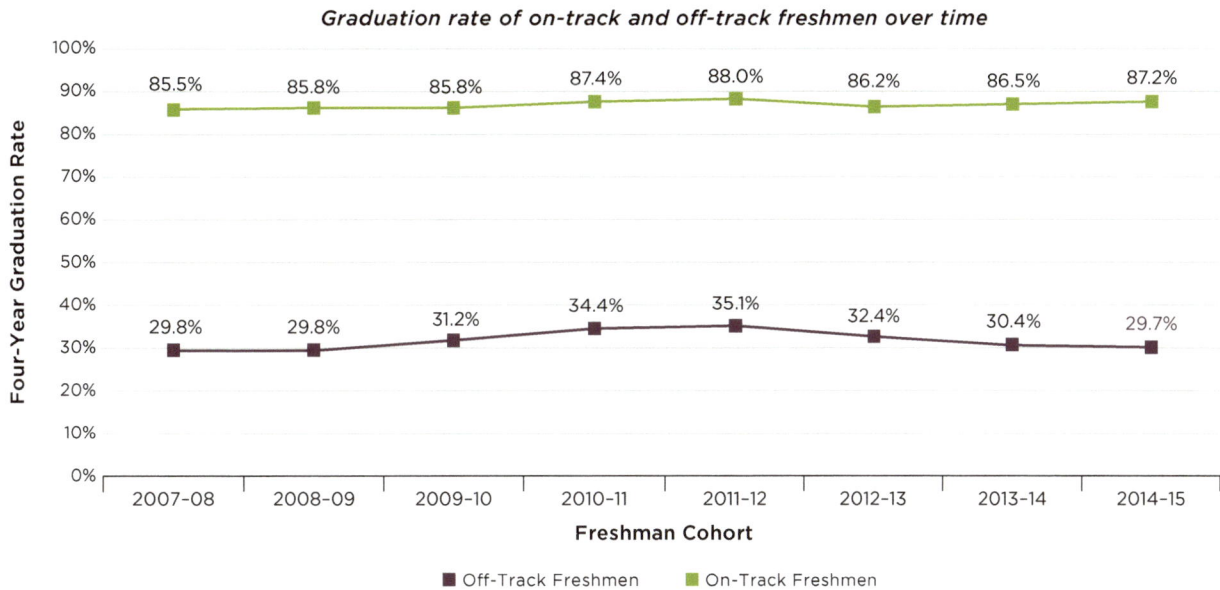

Note: Charter school students are excluded from this analysis. Graduation status is based on whether a student graduated from CPS within four years of starting high school. For more information, see Appendix A.

FIGURE 2

As Graduation and Freshman OnTrack Rates Increased, a Greater Proportion of Non-Graduates Were On-Track as Freshmen

Freshman OnTrack and graduation status by freshman cohort

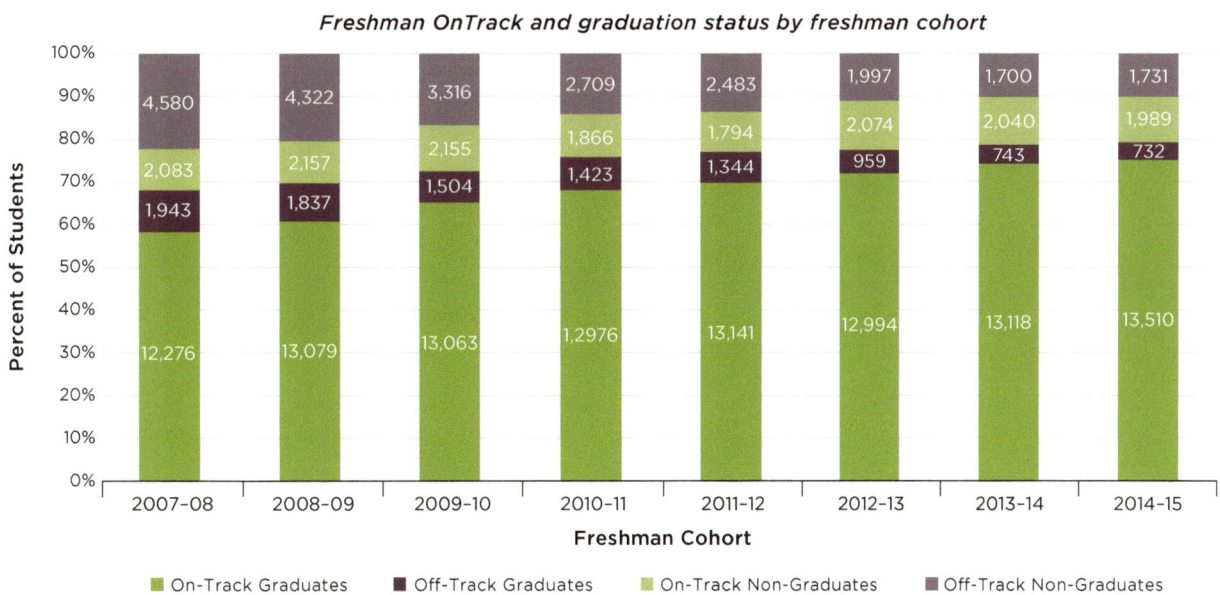

Note: Charter school students are excluded from this analysis. Graduation status is based on whether a student graduated from CPS within four years of starting high school. For more information, see Appendix A.

CHAPTER 2

Sophomore OnTrack in Chicago Public Schools

Sophmore OnTrack

At the end of sophomore year, a CPS student is considered on-track for high school graduation if:

1 They have no more than **1 core course* failure** in tenth grade

&

11 and have **earned 11 credits**, enough to be promoted to eleventh grade

Note: *English, math, science, social studies

Since 2010, CPS has defined and started monitoring Sophomore OnTrack, a sophomore-year indicator of high school graduation. CPS defines Sophomore OnTrack similarly to Freshman OnTrack: in order to be on-track, students must fail no more than one semester of a core course during sophomore year and must accumulate 11 credits by the end of sophomore year. In this way, the Sophomore OnTrack metric incorporates both within-year and cumulative performance; in order to be on-track, sophomore students must pass almost all of their core courses during their sophomore year, but their credit accumulation builds off of the credits they accumulated during their freshman year.

As the district and schools have invested heavily in intentional work around supporting their students as freshmen, they have seen significant gains in their students' sophomore performance as well. The Sophomore OnTrack rate for CPS students has been increasing steadily over time alongside the Freshman OnTrack rate, growing from 61 percent for the 2007–08 freshman cohort to 85 percent for the 2016–17 cohort (**see Figure 3**).

Like Freshman OnTrack, Sophomore OnTrack is highly predictive of high school graduation: only 28 percent of the 2014–15 freshman cohort (graduating class of 2018) who were off-track at the end of sophomore year graduated from high school within four years (**see Figure 4**). However, also like Freshman OnTrack, Sophomore OnTrack does not identify all of the students in danger of not graduating without additional support. In fact, 30 percent of all CPS non-graduates from the 2014–15 freshman cohort (graduating class of 2018) were on-track as sophomores, suggesting that sophomore educators need more nuanced indicators in order to identify the students who need additional support during sophomore year (**see Figure D.2 in Appendix D**).

Although it is not part of the district's accountability system, CPS has integrated Sophomore OnTrack into internal data dashboards and quarterly reporting for all CPS high schools. Sophomore success teams are still less prevalent than freshman success teams, but some schools have expanded freshman success strategies to sophomore year, extending student supports and adopting similar meeting structures in order to monitor sophomore data.

FIGURE 3

Sophomore OnTrack Has Increased Over Time

Sophomore OnTrack rate of CPS freshman cohorts over time

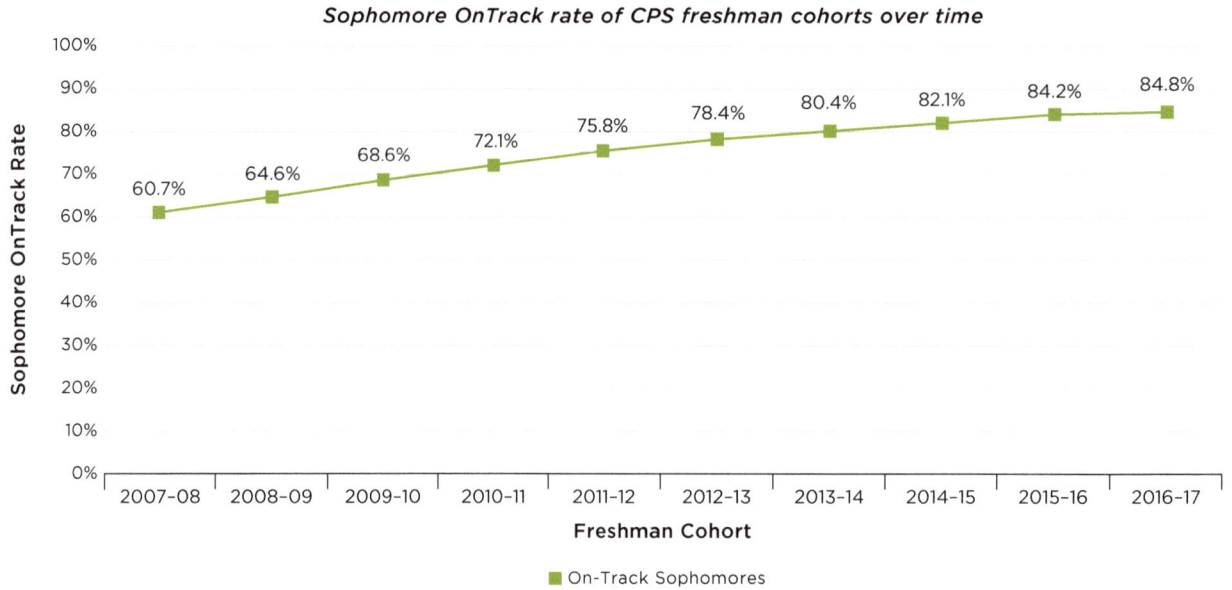

Note: Charter school students are excluded, and only students who were freshmen at CPS are included in sophomore analysis. For more information, see Appendix A.

FIGURE 4

The Predictivity of Sophomore OnTrack Has Held Over Time

Graduation rate of on-track and off-track sophomores over time

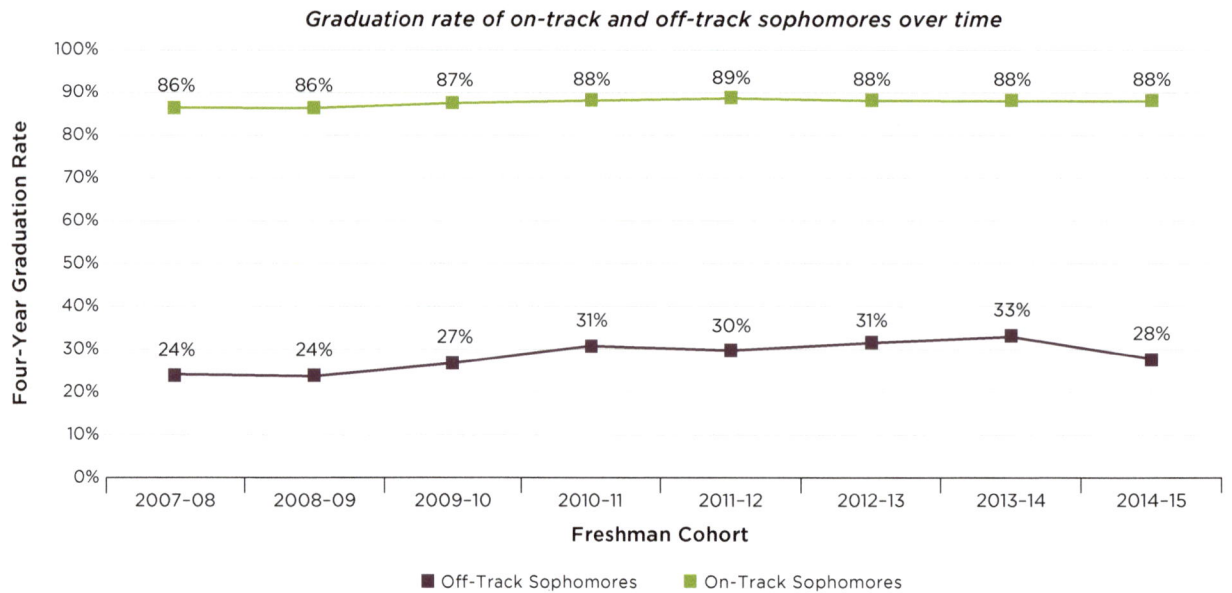

Note: Charter school students are excluded, and only students who were freshmen at CPS are included in sophomore analysis. Graduation status is based on whether a student graduated from CPS within four years of starting high school. For more information, see Appendix A.

Sophomore vs. Freshman Performance on Key Indicators

As more schools expand upon their freshman success strategies and continue the work of supporting students through their subsequent high school years, it is important to understand the relationship between performance in freshman year and performance in sophomore year.

Being on-track as a freshman is highly predictive of being on-track as a sophomore, but it does not guarantee it. Many students fall off-track during sophomore year: almost 8 percent of the students in the 2016–17 freshman cohort were on-track as freshmen, but fell off-track during sophomore year (**see Table 1**). Further, the Sophomore OnTrack rate is lower than the Freshman OnTrack rate because, on average, students' performance declines from freshman to sophomore year. Rates of course failure increase in every subject from freshman to sophomore year, including core subjects (**see Figure 5**).

The course failure rate of the students in this study increased most in math, from 5.0 percent for freshmen to 7.5 percent for sophomores. The failure rate in non-core courses also increased, from 3.8 percent during freshman year to 5.1 percent during sophomore year. This suggests that, although focus and efforts around Freshman OnTrack in CPS high schools appear to have led to some effective student supports and, subsequently, significant gains in both freshman and sophomore outcomes, many students still begin to struggle during sophomore year.

In addition to course failures increasing from freshman to sophomore year, on average, students' grades decline slightly and their attendance declines significantly. The proportion of students in this study with a GPA below 1.5 increased marginally (about one percentage point) from freshman to sophomore year; 13.3 percent of freshmen, compared to 14.4 percent of sophomores, had a GPA below 1.5. There was a larger increase

TABLE 1

Freshman and Sophomore OnTrack Status, 2016-17 Cohort

	On-Track Sophomore	Off-Track Sophomore
On-Track Freshman	**14,100** (82.9% of students)	**1,338** (7.9% of students)
Off-Track Freshman	**316** (1.9% of students)	**1,251** (7.4% of students)

Note: Charter school students are excluded from this analysis. Graduation status is based on whether a student graduated from CPS within four years of starting high school. For more information, see Appendix A.

FIGURE 5

Rates of Course Failure Rose in All Subjects from Freshman to Sophomore Year

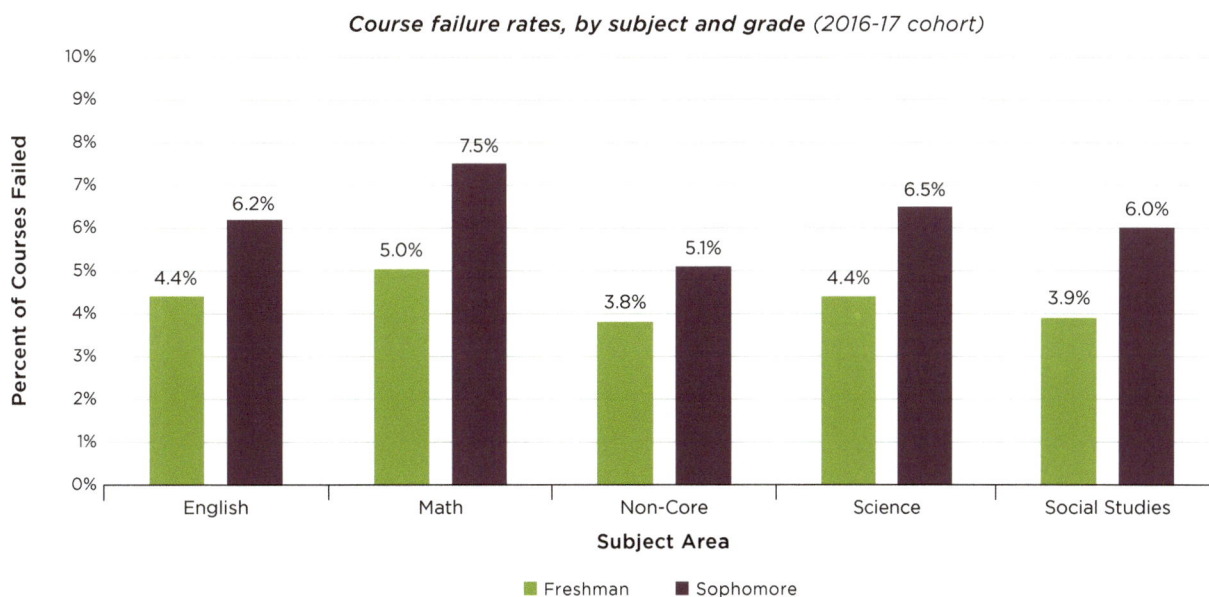

Course failure rates, by subject and grade (2016-17 cohort)

Note: Non-core courses include all courses taken for credit that are not in English, math, science, or social studies. Charter school students are excluded from this analysis, and only students for whom both freshman and sophomore grades were available are inlcuded. For more information, see Appendix A.

(4 percentage points) in the proportion of students with an attendance rate below 80 percent; 9.5 percent of freshmen, compared to 13.7 percent of sophomores, had attendance rates below 80 percent (see Figure 6). This represents hundreds of students whose attendance rate was alarmingly low in their sophomore year, which makes understanding the predictive power of attendance especially important.

Like Freshman OnTrack, Sophomore OnTrack is a powerful but limited indicator of high school outcomes. A student's Freshman OnTrack status and Sophomore OnTrack status reflect important information about their likelihood of graduating from high school (see Appendix D), but they may not reflect other important changes in their performance. Students' course failures, grades, and attendance can change significantly from freshman to sophomore year, and those changes give educators important signals about which students need additional support in order to be successful. Understanding how a more nuanced system of monitoring student performance could help educators better support students will be the focus of the next two chapters.

FIGURE 6

More Students Saw a Decline in Attendance Rates than GPAs from Freshman to Sophomore Year

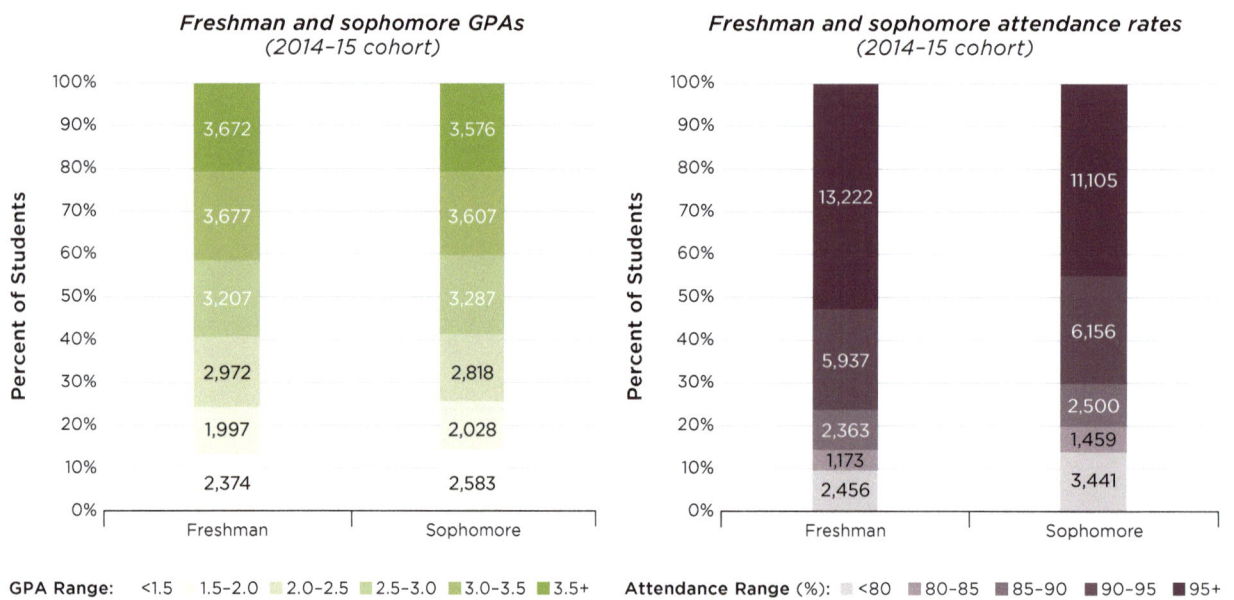

Freshman and sophomore GPAs
(2014–15 cohort)

Freshman and sophomore attendance rates
(2014–15 cohort)

GPA Range: <1.5   1.5-2.0   2.0-2.5   2.5-3.0   3.0-3.5   3.5+

Attendance Range (%): <80   80-85   85-90   90-95   95+

Note: Only students for whom both freshman and sophomore data were available are included in this analysis. Charter students are excluded from the left figure because grade data from charter schools was not available. For more information, see Appendix A.

CHAPTER 3

Freshman Indicators for Sophomore Educators

Freshman Warning Indicators

Three key freshman warning indicators suggest a need for support or intervention during sophomore year:

Off-track status at the end of freshman year

<85% **Freshman attendance** below 85%

F A **course failure** in any course during freshman year

The success of Freshman OnTrack work at CPS has been enabled in part by freshman educators' use of two forms of data to implement supports for students. First, at the beginning of the year, freshman educators use information about their incoming students' eighth-grade attendance and grades, which prior research shows are the most accurate predictors of high school performance.[3] Second, during freshman year, freshman educators are able to monitor their students' Freshman OnTrack status, freshman grades, and freshman attendance over the course of the school year. In order to work most effectively with their students, sophomore educators also need indicators that enable them to 1) understand the academic status of their incoming cohorts and to 2) monitor students' progress throughout the school year.

Freshman OnTrack remains a critical indicator of high school graduation with applications for both freshman and sophomore educators. However, as we have seen, Freshman OnTrack does not identify all students who are in danger of not graduating. Making more nuanced freshman indicators available to sophomore educators at the beginning of the school year could help them identify more students who are likely to need additional support during sophomore year in order to stay on-track to graduation.

In thinking about what indicators sophomore educators might use to understand their incoming students, we need to consider what indicators are available to sophomore educators at the beginning of sophomore year, and which of those are predictive of high school graduation and college enrollment. Freshman OnTrack is not the only measure of freshman performance that is closely related to high school graduation. Even among freshmen who are on-track, freshman course failures and attendance rates are highly predictive of high school graduation, and freshman GPAs are highly predictive of post-secondary outcomes.

A course failure in any freshman course is one indicator that sophomore educators can use to identify on-track students who are in danger of seeing their performance decline during sophomore year without additional support. Freshman OnTrack largely reflects freshman performance in core courses: in order to be off-track, students must fail multiple core courses or fail to accumulate at least five total credits. Most students who pass all, or all but one, of their core courses during freshman year earn a status of on-track, even if they failed multiple non-core courses. However, students' experiences in all their freshman courses, not just their core courses, matter for their likelihood

---

3 Allensworth et al. (2014).

Selecting Effective Indicators for Sophomore Educators

What makes an indicator effective? Previous research has shown that the most effective indicators in educational settings share five key characteristics:[G]

- **Predictiveness**
- **Usability and clarity**
- **Real-time/right-time availability**
- **Direct causal link to outcomes that matter**
- **Malleability**

In selecting a useful indicator of non-graduation for sophomore educators, maximizing predictiveness involves weighing an important trade-off: we want **1)** to identify as many students as possible who may need additional support and **2)** to avoid misidentifying students as needing further support so that we can better target interventions to the students who could most benefit from them. In technical terms, that means we want to find indicators with both 1) *high identification rates* and 2) low *false positive rates*.

For an indicator that predicts non-graduation, the *identification rate* is the proportion of the eventual non-graduates that it correctly flags as in danger of not graduating from high school during their sophomore year. The *false positive rate* is the proportion of the eventual graduates that it incorrectly flags as in danger of not graduating. Most indicators that flag a large number of students have a high identification rate and a high false positive rate. In other words, they identify most eventual non-graduates, but also incorrectly flag many students who do graduate. As a result, an educator using one of these indicators might not be able to target limited resource-intensive

supports to only the students who need them most. On the other hand, most indicators that identify a small number of students have a low false positive rate and a low identification rate, meaning that they correctly identify almost exclusively non-graduates, but also fail to identify many non-graduates. An educator using one of these indicators might miss certain students who are in need of additional support.

The most useful possible indicator of non-graduation would have a high identification rate—correctly identifying almost all of the eventual non-graduates—but a low false positive rate—incorrectly flagging very few eventual graduates as requiring extra support. This indicator would allow educators to target supports and interventions to the students in significant danger of not graduating from high school without additional support.

Of course, no indicator will be perfect, and this is a good thing, because it reflects the fact that a student's fate is not determined at the end of freshman or sophomore year; with the right support, students who are off-track at the end of freshman year can get back on-track to graduation.

Freshman and Sophomore OnTrack are effective indicators because of their low false positive rates; they enable schools to funnel resources to a relatively small group of students who are likely to require significant supports in order to graduate from high school. Additional indicators, particularly those with higher identification rates, could further support sophomore educators' work by identifying additional students who could also benefit from supports and interventions during sophomore year.

G   Allensworth, Nagaoka, & Johnson (2018).

---

of graduation (**see Figure C.1 in Appendix C**). Thus, an F in any course during freshman year may signal a need for additional support during sophomore year.

Low freshman attendance is another powerful indicator of non-graduation, even for students who pass all of their freshman courses. A freshman attendance rate below 85 percent is roughly as predictive of non-graduation as an off-track status (**see Figure D.1 in Appendix D**). Freshman attendance is important, in part because it is directly related to students' freshman grades (**see Figure 7**), but freshman attendance is also independently predictive of high school graduation, meaning

that it predicts high school graduation even among students who earned similar grades. For example, among students with a freshman GPA between 2.0 and 2.5, more than 90 percent of students with an attendance rate of at least 95 percent went on to graduate from high school within four years, while the graduation rate for students with an attendance rate of 80-85 percent who earned similar grades was 59 percent (**see Figure 8**).

All three of these warning indicators—an off-track status, freshman attendance below 85 percent, and any freshman course failure—are powerful warning indicators of non-graduation for incoming sophomores.

FIGURE 7

Freshman Year Attendance and GPA Are Closely Related

Freshman GPA, by freshman attendance (2016–17 cohort)

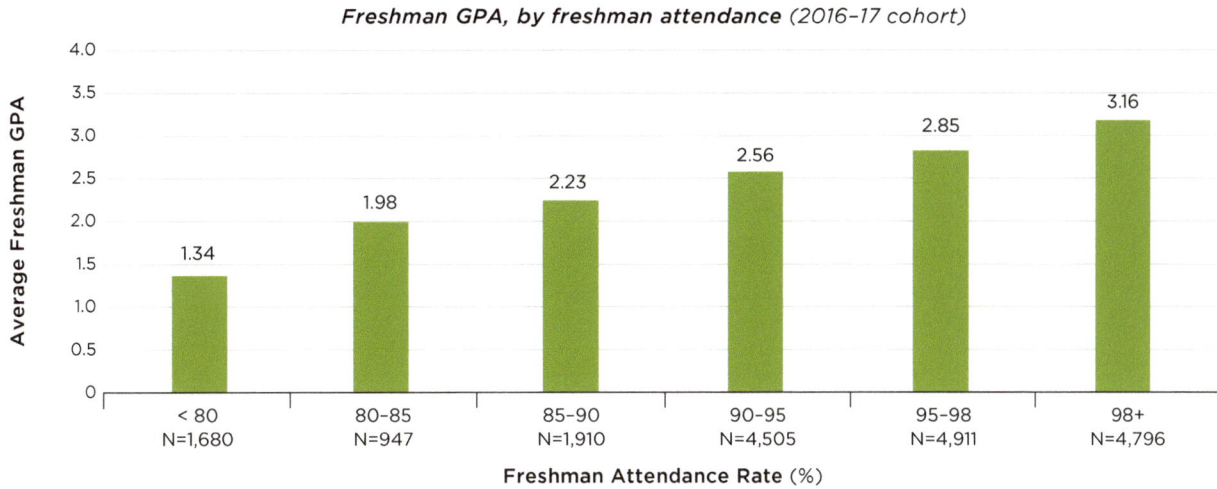

Note: Charter school students are excluded from this analysis. For more information, see Appendix A.

FIGURE 8

Even Among Students with Similar GPAs, Freshman Attendance Is Highly Predictive of Graduation

High school graduation, by freshman GPA and attendance category (2014–15 cohort)

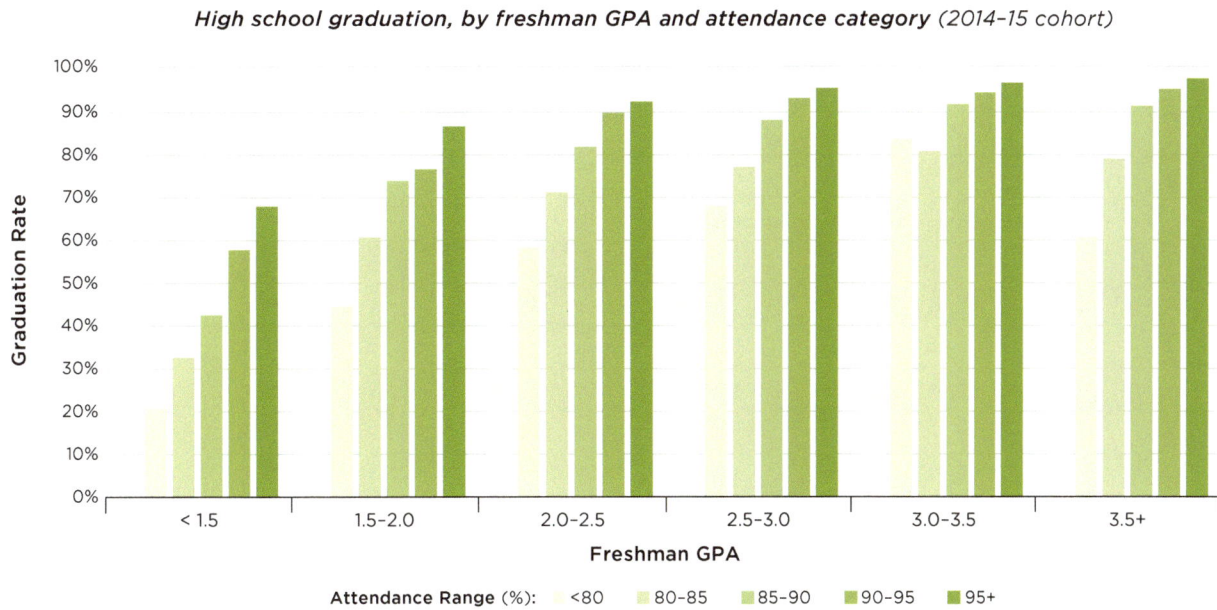

Note: Charter school students are excluded from this analysis. Graduation status is based on whether a student graduated from CPS within four years of starting high school. For more information, see Appendix A.

Together, they identify most (70 percent) of the incoming sophomores who did not go on to graduate (**see Figure 9**). It's important to note that with the right supports, some students who struggle during freshman year do get back on-track and persist to graduation: 17 percent of 2018 graduates had one or more warning indicators at the end of their freshman year. Access to more nuanced warning indicators at the beginning of sophomore year could help sophomore educators identify more of the students who need these supports early in the school year.

In addition to keeping students on-track for high school graduation, another important goal of many sophomore educators is preparing students to enroll in

college after graduation. Earning a GPA of at least 3.0 in high school—at least a B average—expands CPS students' access to a broad range of post-secondary opportunities, including eligibility for the Chicago STAR scholarship and more likely admission to selective and highly-selective colleges. Previous Consortium research has established freshman GPA as a critical indicator of eleventh-grade GPA, high school graduation, college enrollment, and college retention.[4] Among freshman outcomes, course failures and attendance are the most powerful warning indicators for high school graduation, but GPA is the most powerful indicator of college access and enrollment.

By using an indicator system that combines all of these key predictive indicators—a GPA threshold of 3.0, in addition to the three warning indicators for high school graduation—sophomore educators could differentiate their students in ways that would allow them to identify their students' potential challenges, and effectively target supports for them. **Table A (see *Freshman Success Categories* box on p.17)** offers a set of indicator categories for incoming sophomores; it supplements students' Freshman OnTrack status with additional information about their freshman course failures, attendance, and GPAs. This system contains four Freshman Success Categories: 1) Off-Track, 2) On-Track Warning, 3) On-Track Below 3.0, and 4) On-Track Above 3.0. These categories identify four distinct groups of incoming sophomores who may need different kinds of supports during sophomore year.

FIGURE 9

Around 70 Percent of Non-Graduates Had at Least One Warning Indicator at the End of Freshman Year

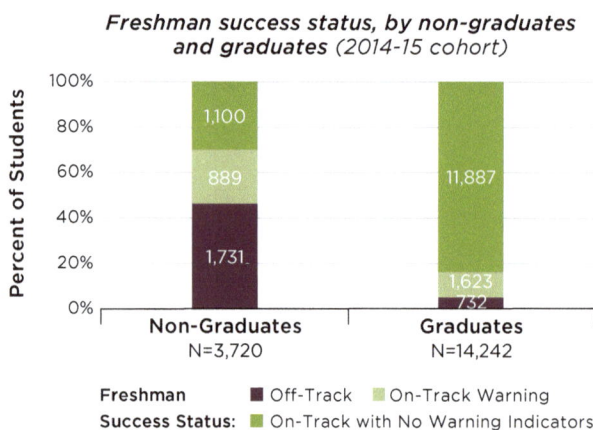

Freshman success status, by non-graduates and graduates (2014-15 cohort)

Note: This figure shows the freshman warning indicators of 2014–15 freshmen broken down by their their graduation status in 2018. Charter school students are excluded from this analysis. For more information, see Appendix A.

---

4   Easton et al. (2017).

Freshman Success Categories: Definitions and Predictivity

On-Track Above 3.0 Students in the On-Track Above 3.0 category were on-track, passed all of their sophomore courses, had an attendance rate above 85 percent, and earned at least a 3.0 GPA during freshman year. Almost all (95 percent) of the 6,545 students in this group went on to graduate high school within four years, 80 percent immediately enrolled in college post-graduation, and 64 percent immediately enrolled in a four-year college post-graduation. It is important for incoming sophomores in the On-Track Above 3.0 group to maintain their strong grades sophomore year in order to stay on-track for access to selective and highly-selective post-secondary opportunities.

On-Track Below 3.0 This category includes students who were on-track, passed all of their courses, had a freshman attendance rate above 85 percent, and earned a GPA below 3.0. Of the 5,780 students in this group, 88 percent went on to graduate from high school within four years, 58 percent enrolled immediately in college after graduation, and 32 percent enrolled immediately in a four-year college after graduation. Students who end freshman year in this group may need additional support in improving their performance during sophomore year in order to increase both their likelihood of enrolling in college and their level of access to selective and highly-selective post-secondary opportunities.

On-Track Warning Students who were on-track but had a freshman attendance rate below 85 percent or who failed a course in any subject are classified as On-Track Warning. Despite being on-track as freshmen, the 2,833 students who were in the On-Track Warning group graduated from high school at a rate of 64 percent, enrolled immediately in college at a rate of 36 percent, and enrolled immediately in a four-year college at a rate of 16 percent (**see Figure 10**). The course failures or low attendance of students in this category may indicate a need for additional support during sophomore year in order to stay on-track for graduation and college enrollment.

Off-Track Off-track freshmen are those who failed at least two semesters of a core course or did not accumulate five credits by the end of freshman year. The 2,443 off-track students in the 2013–14 freshman cohort graduated from high school at a rate of 30 percent.[H] The students in this group immediately enrolled in college at a rate of 16 percent and immediately enrolled in a four-year college at a rate of 6 percent (**see Figure 10**). Students who end freshman year off-track likely require significant interventions during sophomore year, including credit recovery opportunities and individualized supports, to get back on-track to graduate from high school and enroll in college.

TABLE A

Freshman Success Categories

Category	Indicators	Students (2013–14 Cohort)
On-Track Above 3.0	• On-track; • Above 3.0 GPA; • No Fs; and • Above 85% attendance	6,545
On-Track Below 3.0	• On-track; • Below 3.0 GPA; • No Fs; and • Above 85% attendance	5,780
On-Track Warning	• On-track; • At least one F; or • Below 85% attendance	2,833
Off-Track	• 2+ Core Fs; or • Below 5 credits accumulated	2,443

Note: Charter school students are not included in this table. For more information, see Appendix A.

[H] All Freshman Success Categories outcomes analyses were conducted using the 2013–14 freshman cohort, so that we could include college enrollment outcomes in addition to high school graduation outcomes.

FIGURE 10

Student Outcomes by Freshman Success Category

High school graduation and college enrollment rates, by Freshman Success Category (2013–14 cohort)

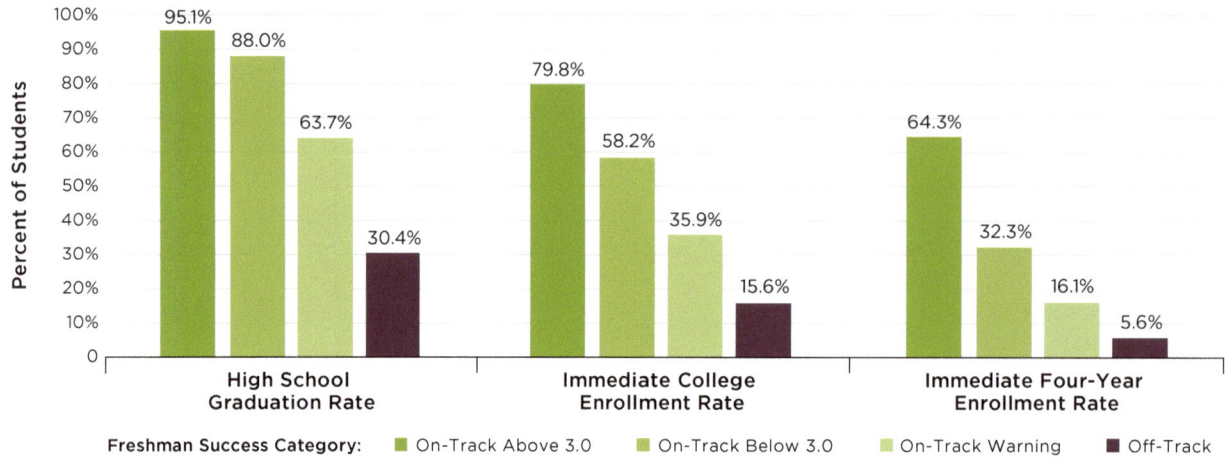

Note: Charter school students are excluded from this analysis. Graduation status is based on whether a student graduated from CPS within four years of starting high school. For more information, see Appendix A.

CHAPTER 4

Sophomore Indicators for Sophomore Educators

Sophomore Warning Indicators

Three key sophomore warning indicators suggest a need for support or intervention:

Sophomore Off-track status at the end of sophomore year

<85% **Sophomore attendance** below 85%

F A **course failure** in any course during sophomore year

Together, freshman and sophomore performance provide sophomore educators with a great deal of information about students' likelihood of graduating from high school and enrolling in college. By the end of sophomore year, most students have earned around half of the grades that will contribute to their graduating GPA, and two-thirds of the grades that will be included in their college applications. Sophomore educators have the benefit of additional information about their students' performance and, as a result, have even more performance measures to choose from than freshman educators, though they often receive less guidance about which measures are most important to monitor during the school year. In addition to Freshman Success Categories, which enable them to understand the prior academic success of their incoming students, sophomore educators may also benefit from having Sophomore Success Categories that enable them to monitor their students' performance on key indicators during sophomore year.

In this section, we explore the predictivity of sophomore indicators of graduation and college enrollment and offer a set of Sophomore Success Categories for sophomore educators. Unsurprisingly, there is a high degree of symmetry between freshman and sophomore indicators that are predictive of high school graduation. All three of the powerful warning indicators of high school graduation in freshman year—off-track status, attendance below 85 percent, and any course failures—

remain highly predictive of non-graduation for sophomores (**see Figures C.2 and D.2 in Appendices C and D**).

Sophomore attendance is a particularly strong predictor of students' likelihood of graduating from high school. Like freshman attendance, sophomore attendance was both highly predictive of students' GPAs (**see Figure 11**) and predictive of high school graduation, even among students who earned similar GPAs (**see Figure 12**). As we have seen, on average, students' attendance declines significantly from freshman to sophomore year, more precipitously than do their grades. Because low sophomore attendance is a warning indicator even for students with strong sophomore grades, monitoring attendance presents schools with an opportunity to identify and support students who are earning strong grades, but are still in danger of not graduating from high school without additional support.

Nearly all students from the 2014–15 freshman cohort who did not graduate from high school within four years (by spring 2018) showed at least one of these warning indicators—an off-track status, attendance rate below 85 percent, or course failure—by the end of sophomore year of high school (**see Figure 13**). In total, 84 percent of these students had a warning flag as sophomores: 63 percent were off-track, and an additional 21 percent had either an attendance rate below 85 percent

FIGURE 11

Sophomore Attendance Is Related to Sophomore GPA

Sophomore GPA, by sophomore attendance (2016-17 cohort)

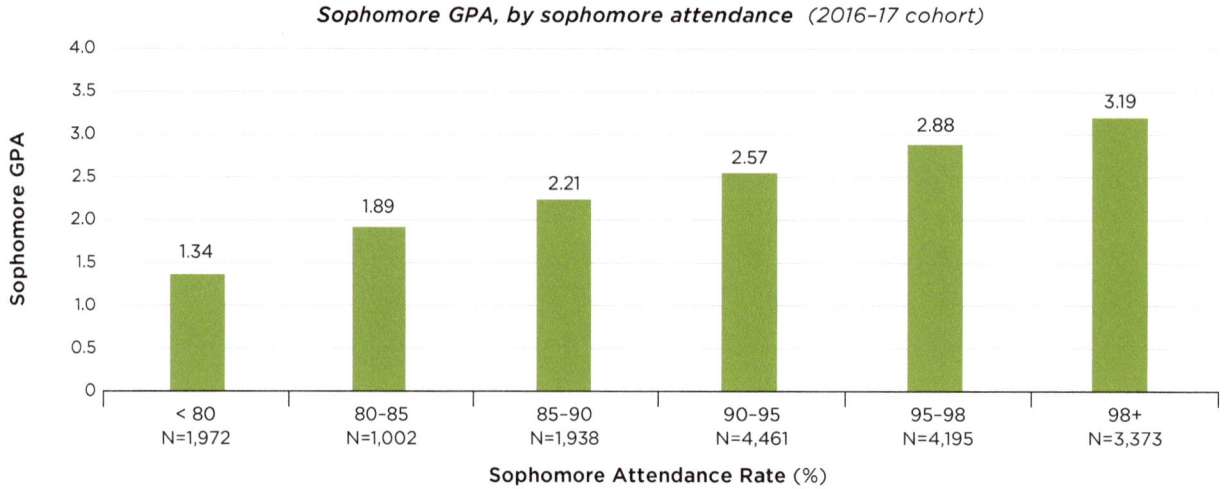

Note: Only students who were freshmen at CPS are included in sophomore analysis. Charter students are also excluded. For more information, see Appendix A.

FIGURE 12

Even Among Students with Similar GPAs, Sophomore Attendance Is Highly Predictive of Graduation

High school graduation, by sophomore GPA and attendance category (2014-15 cohort)

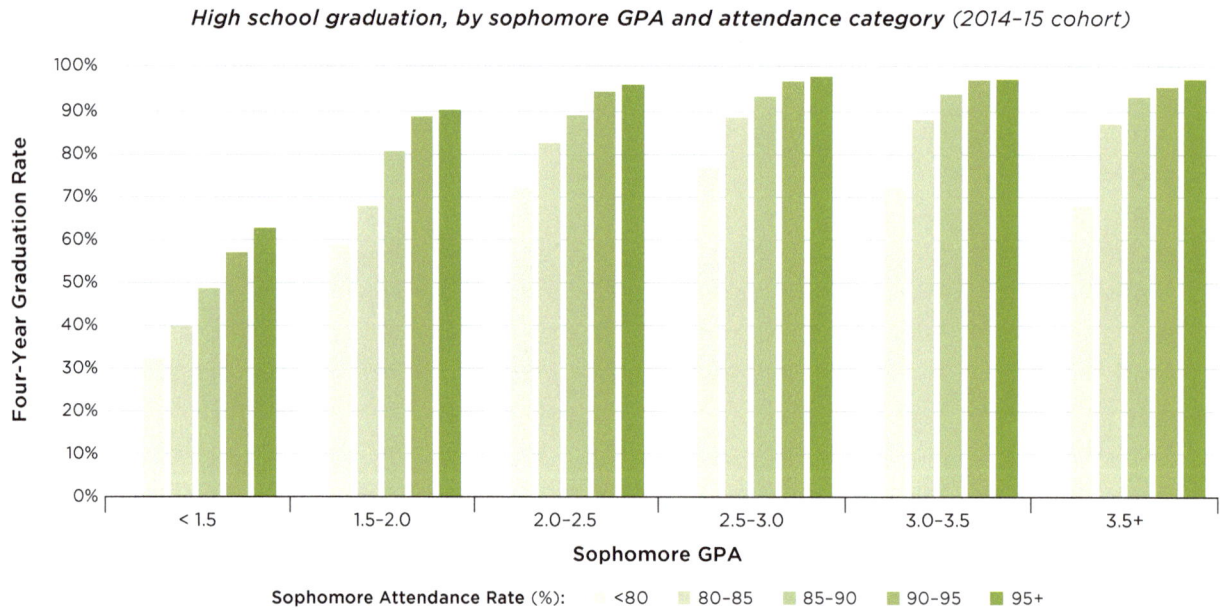

Sophomore Attendance Rate (%):   <80   80-85   85-90   90-95   95+

Note: Only students who were freshmen at CPS are included in sophomore analysis. Charter students are also excluded. Graduation status is based on whether a student graduated from CPS within four years of starting high school. For more information, see Appendix A.

a or at least one course failure during sophomore year. By targeting additional resources to the students who begin to struggle for the first time during sophomore year, sophomore educators can keep more students on-track for graduation and college enrollment.

Table B (see *Sophomore Success Categories* box on p.22) contains an indicator system for sophomore outcomes, based on within-sophomore-year performance that incorporates students' Sophomore OnTrack status, attendance, GPA, and course failures. Like the Freshman Success Categories, the Sophomore Success Categories include one category for off-track students (Off-Track), and divide the remaining on-track students into three groups based on their within-year sophomore attendance and course performance: 1) On-Track Warning, 2) On-Track Below 3.0, and 3) On-Track Above 3.0.

Fewer than 20 Percent of Non-Graduates Were On-Track with No Warning Indicators during Sophomore Year

Sophomore success status, by non-graduates and graduates (2014-15 cohort)

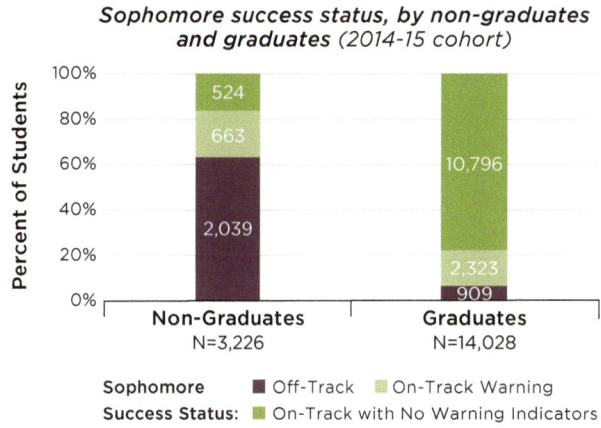

Non-Graduates N=3,226	Graduates N=14,028
Off-Track: 2,039	Off-Track: 909
On-Track Warning: 663	On-Track Warning: 2,323
On-Track with No Warning Indicators: 524	On-Track with No Warning Indicators: 10,796

Sophomore Success Status: ■ Off-Track ■ On-Track Warning ■ On-Track with No Warning Indicators

Note: This figure shows the sophomore warning indicators of 2014–15 freshmen broken down by their their graduation status in 2018. Only students who were freshmen at CPS are included in sophomore analysis. Charter students are also excluded. For more information, see Appendix A.

FIGURE 14

Student Outcomes by Sophomore Success Category

High school graduation and college enrollment rates, by Sophomore Success Category (2013–14 cohort)

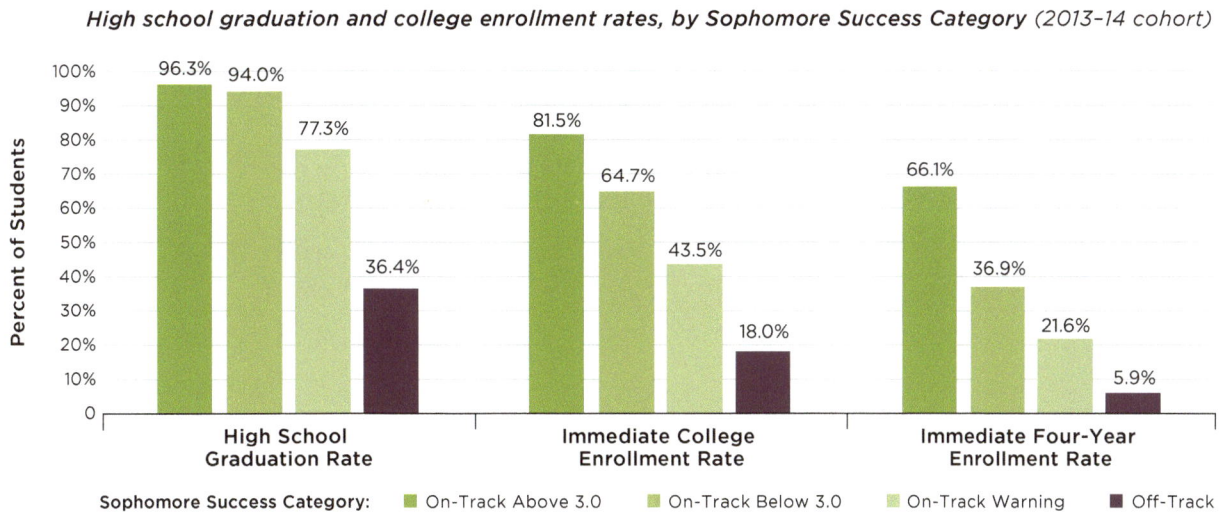

	High School Graduation Rate	Immediate College Enrollment Rate	Immediate Four-Year Enrollment Rate
On-Track Above 3.0	96.3%	81.5%	66.1%
On-Track Below 3.0	94.0%	64.7%	36.9%
On-Track Warning	77.3%	43.5%	21.6%
Off-Track	36.4%	18.0%	5.9%

Sophomore Success Category: ■ On-Track Above 3.0 ■ On-Track Below 3.0 ■ On-Track Warning ■ Off-Track

Note: Only students who were freshmen at CPS are included in sophomore analysis. Charter students are also excluded. Graduation status is based on whether a student graduated from CPS within four years of starting high school. For more information, see Appendix A.

Sophomore Success Categories: Definitions and Predictivity

On-Track Above 3.0 Students in the On-Track Above 3.0 category were on-track, passed all of their sophomore courses, had an attendance rate above 85 percent, and earned at least a 3.0 GPA during sophomore year. The 6,116 students in this group graduated from high school within four years at a rate of 96 percent, immediately enrolled in college at a rate of 82 percent, and immediately enrolled in a four-year college at a rate of 66 percent. The high rates of college enrollment for the On-Track Above 3.0 students highlights the importance of a GPA of at least 3.0 during both freshman and sophomore year.

On-Track Below 3.0 Students in the On-Track Below 3.0 category were on-track, passed all of their sophomore courses, had an attendance rate above 85 percent, and earned a GPA below 3.0 during sophomore year. While the 4,777 students in this group graduated from high school at a high rate of 94 percent, they immediately enrolled in college at a rate of 65 percent, and immediately enrolled in a four-year college at a rate of 37 percent, a much lower rate than their peers who earned a GPA of at least 3.0 as sophomores.

On-Track Warning Students in the On-Track Warning category were on-track, but had an attendance rate below 85 percent or failed at least one course in any subject. Although these students were on-track, their low attendance or course failures suggest that they may need additional support during sophomore year to stay on-track for high school graduation. The 2,761 students in this group graduated from high school at a rate of 77 percent, immediately enrolled in college at a rate of 44 percent, and immediately enrolled in a four-year college at a rate of 22 percent.

Off-Track Off-Track sophomores likely require significant supports and interventions in order to graduate from high school within four years. The 3,147 students (from the 2013-14 cohort of freshmen) in this category at the end of their sophomore year graduated from high school at a rate of 36.4 percent and enrolled immediately in a four-year college at a rate of 5.9 percent (**see Figure 14 on p.21**).[I]

TABLE B
Sophomore Success Categories

Category	Indicators	Students (2013–14 Cohort)
On-Track Above 3.0	• On-track; • Above 3.0 GPA; • No Fs; and • Above 85% attendance	6,116
On-Track Below 3.0	• On-track; • Below 3.0 GPA; • No Fs; and • Above 85% attendance	4,777
On-Track Warning	• On-track; • At least one F; or • Below 85% attendance	2,761
Off-Track	• 2+ Core Fs; or • Below 5 credits accumulated	3,147

Note: Charter school students are not included in this table. For more information, see Appendix A.

I   All Sophomore Success Categories outcomes analyses were conducted using the 2013–14 freshman cohort, so that we could include college enrollment outcomes in addition to high school graduation outcomes. Data reported here are from outcomes at the end of students' sophomore year.

CHAPTER 5

Freshman and Sophomore Trajectories

Chapters 1–4 illustrate that both freshman and sophomore success are highly predictive of students' high school outcomes and college enrollment. In this chapter, we explore students' high school and college outcomes based on their Freshman and Sophomore Success Categories. We break down sophomore success by race/ethnicity and gender, and also examine in more detail how freshman and sophomore success are related. Understanding the relationship between freshman and sophomore performance, and the strong relationship between sophomore success and high school and college outcomes, can inform sophomore educators' work to improve students' educational trajectories.

As Freshman OnTrack and Sophomore OnTrack rates have increased over the past decade, students' performance on other freshman and sophomore indicators has also improved. In 2008, nearly 40 percent of the 2007–08 freshman cohort were off-track as sophomores; 20 percent earned a 3.0 GPA or higher during their sophomore year. A decade later, in 2016, only 15 percent of the freshman cohort were off-track during sophomore year, and more than 40 percent earned a GPA of 3.0 or higher as sophomores (**see Figure 15**). These improvements largely mirror the gains in Freshman OnTrack, suggesting that investments in freshman year have led to gains in sophomore performance as well.

However, the gains in sophomore performance have not been experienced equally by all groups of students, suggesting that not all students are receiving the supports that they need to be successful during sophomore year. In particular, 21 percent of Latino young men and 22 percent of Black young men in the 2016–17 freshman cohort were off-track at the end of sophomore year (**see Figure 16**). Moreover, only 30 percent of Latino young men and only 20 percent of Black young men earned a GPA of 3.0 or higher during their sophomore year. This is important, in part because a 3.0 GPA has critical implications for students' access to selective and highly-

selective colleges and other post-secondary pathways. If Black and Latino young men aren't getting the supports that they need to be successful during the first two years of high school, they will not have access to as broad a range of post-secondary opportunities as their peers.

Trajectories through Success Categories

Both freshman and sophomore success indicators are highly predictive of students' high school graduation, but there is still a high degree of movement between Freshman and Sophomore Success Categories. Many freshmen who were on-track with less than a 3.0 GPA began to show signs of struggle during sophomore year, and some students who were off-track during freshman year were able to get back on-track with strong sophomore performance. Specifically, 25 percent of the 2013–14 freshman cohort fell at least one category from freshman to sophomore year, and 14 percent moved up at least one category (**see Figure 17**).

Freshmen in the On-Track Above 3.0 and Off-Track categories were relatively unlikely to see their performance change significantly during sophomore year. Most students who earned a 3.0 or higher during freshman year continued to earn at least a 3.0 GPA in sophomore year, with only 427 (6 percent) falling to the On-Track Warning category and only 1 percent (60) falling to the Off-Track category during sophomore year.

Likewise, most students who were off-track as freshmen continued to struggle during sophomore year, although some off-track students were able to get back on-track during sophomore year and improve their performance significantly: 266 students (12 percent) moved up to the On-Track Warning category, and an additional 221 (10 percent) moved up to On-Track Below 3.0 or On-Track Above 3.0.

For freshmen in the On-Track Below 3.0 and On-Track Warning categories, sophomore outcomes were much more varied. Of On-Track Below 3.0 freshmen—

FIGURE 15

Freshman and Sophomore Success Rates at CPS Increased over the Past Decade

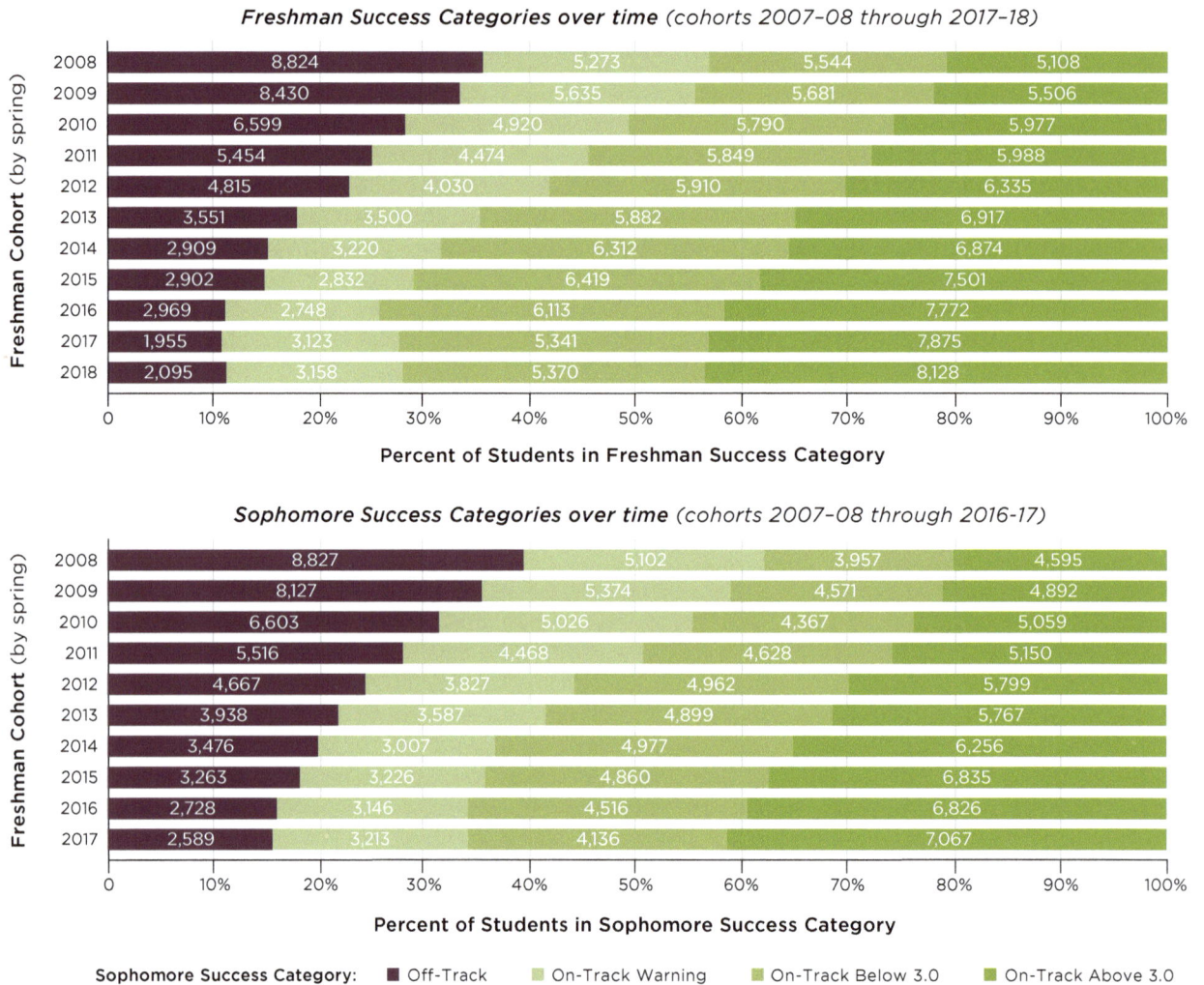

Freshman Success Categories over time (cohorts 2007–08 through 2017–18)

Freshman Cohort (by spring)	Off-Track	On-Track Warning	On-Track Below 3.0	On-Track Above 3.0
2008	8,824	5,273	5,544	5,108
2009	8,430	5,635	5,681	5,506
2010	6,599	4,920	5,790	5,977
2011	5,454	4,474	5,849	5,988
2012	4,815	4,030	5,910	6,335
2013	3,551	3,500	5,882	6,917
2014	2,909	3,220	6,312	6,874
2015	2,902	2,832	6,419	7,501
2016	2,969	2,748	6,113	7,772
2017	1,955	3,123	5,341	7,875
2018	2,095	3,158	5,370	8,128

Percent of Students in Freshman Success Category

Sophomore Success Categories over time (cohorts 2007–08 through 2016-17)

Freshman Cohort (by spring)	Off-Track	On-Track Warning	On-Track Below 3.0	On-Track Above 3.0
2008	8,827	5,102	3,957	4,595
2009	8,127	5,374	4,571	4,892
2010	6,603	5,026	4,367	5,059
2011	5,516	4,468	4,628	5,150
2012	4,667	3,827	4,962	5,799
2013	3,938	3,587	4,899	5,767
2014	3,476	3,007	4,977	6,256
2015	3,263	3,226	4,860	6,835
2016	2,728	3,146	4,516	6,826
2017	2,589	3,213	4,136	7,067

Percent of Students in Sophomore Success Category

Sophomore Success Category: ■ Off-Track ■ On-Track Warning ■ On-Track Below 3.0 ■ On-Track Above 3.0

Note: Only students who were freshmen at CPS are included in sophomore analysis. Charter students are also excluded. For more information, see Appendix A.

FIGURE 16

About One in Five Black and Latino Young Men Were Off-Track at the End of Sophomore Year

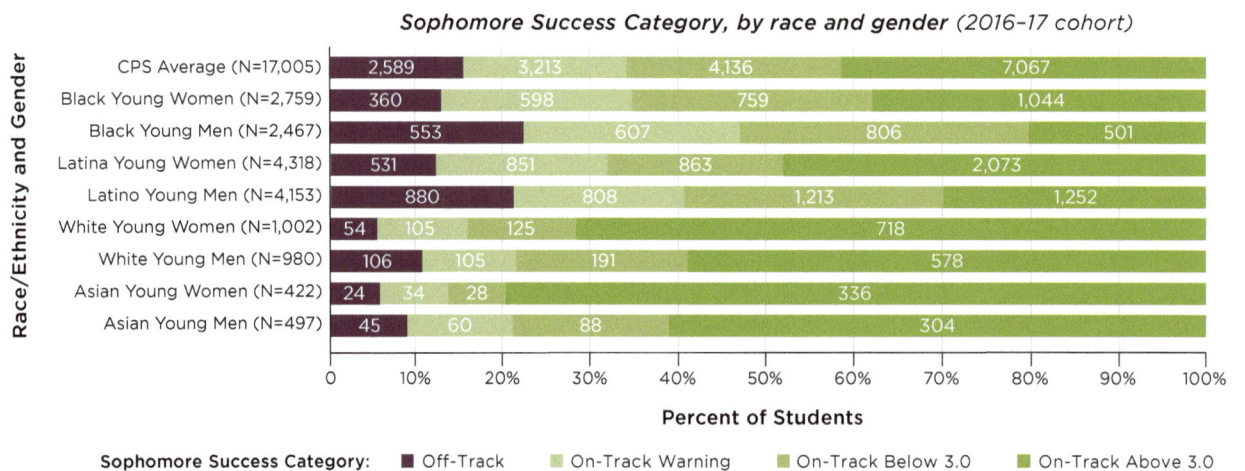

Sophomore Success Category, by race and gender (2016–17 cohort)

Race/Ethnicity and Gender	Off-Track	On-Track Warning	On-Track Below 3.0	On-Track Above 3.0
CPS Average (N=17,005)	2,589	3,213	4,136	7,067
Black Young Women (N=2,759)	360	598	759	1,044
Black Young Men (N=2,467)	553	607	806	501
Latina Young Women (N=4,318)	531	851	863	2,073
Latino Young Men (N=4,153)	880	808	1,213	1,252
White Young Women (N=1,002)	54	105	125	718
White Young Men (N=980)	106	105	191	578
Asian Young Women (N=422)	24	34	28	336
Asian Young Men (N=497)	45	60	88	304

Percent of Students

Sophomore Success Category: ■ Off-Track ■ On-Track Warning ■ On-Track Below 3.0 ■ On-Track Above 3.0

Note: Only students who were freshmen at CPS are included in sophomore analysis. Charter students are also excluded. For more information, see Appendix A.

FIGURE 17

Many Students Changed Success Categories between Freshman and Sophomore Year

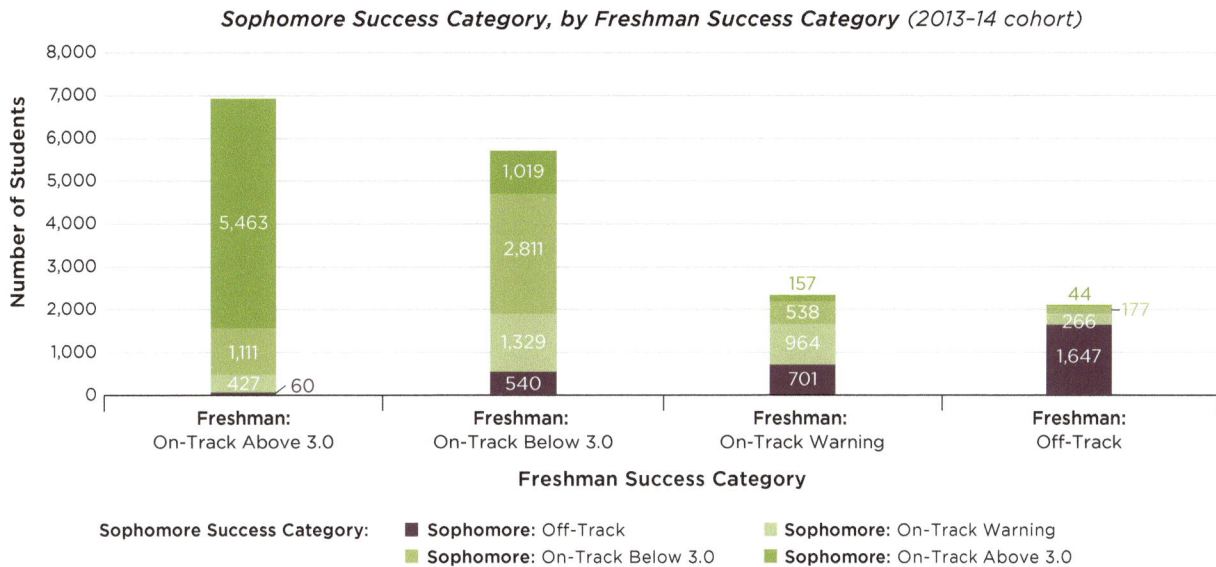

Sophomore Success Category, by Freshman Success Category (2013-14 cohort)

Note: Only students who were freshmen at CPS are included in sophomore analysis. Charter students are also excluded. For more information, see Appendix A.

those who passed all of their courses, had an attendance rate of at least 85 percent, and a GPA below 3.0—1,019 (18 percent) moved up to On-Track Above 3.0 category as sophomores, earning a GPA of 3.0 or higher for the first time. However, 1,869 students (33 percent) fell into the On-Track Warning or the Off-Track categories during sophomore year. Among students who ended freshman year in the On-Track Warning category, 701 (30 percent) fell off-track during sophomore year, 964 (41 percent) remained in the On-Track Warning category, and 695 (29 percent) moved up to On-Track Below 3.0 or On-Track Above 3.0.

Perhaps most notably, nearly one-half of the students who were off-track at the end of sophomore year had been on-track at the end of freshman year: of the 3,147 students in the 2013–14 freshman cohort who were off-track at the end of sophomore year, 1,542 (49 percent) were in either the On-Track Warning, On-Track Below 3.0, or On-Track Above 3.0 categories as freshmen. Students from all demographic categories fell from one success category in freshman year to a lower one in sophomore year (**see Figure 18**).

The degree of movement between Freshman and Sophomore Success Categories signals that although Freshman OnTrack remains a critical indicator of student outcomes, students' educational trajectories are not

fixed at the end of freshman year. With the right supports, students who struggle during freshman year can get back on-track to high school graduation and college enrollment. However, when critical supports fall away between freshman and sophomore year, students who were on-track during freshman year can begin to struggle, sometimes falling off-track for high school graduation.

Students' freshman and sophomore success both matter for their likelihood of graduating from high school and enrolling in college. **Table 2** displays students' graduation rates based on their Freshman and Sophomore OnTrack status. Overall, students who were on-track both freshman and sophomore year graduated at a rate of 93 percent. And students who were on-track freshman year but off-track sophomore year graduated from high school at a rate of 43 percent.

Even for students with very strong freshman performance, warning indicators based on attendance and course failures in sophomore year indicated significant possibility of not graduating from high school without additional support. **Figure 19** displays students' graduation rates based on their Freshman and Sophomore Success Categories. Students who were in the On-Track Below 3.0 or On-Track Above 3.0 categories as freshmen, but struggled and fell off-track during sophomore year, graduated at a rate only slightly greater than 50 percent.

FIGURE 18

Students from Every Demographic Group Fell Off-Track for the First Time during Sophomore Year

Freshman and Sophomore OnTrack status, by race and gender (2016–17 cohort)

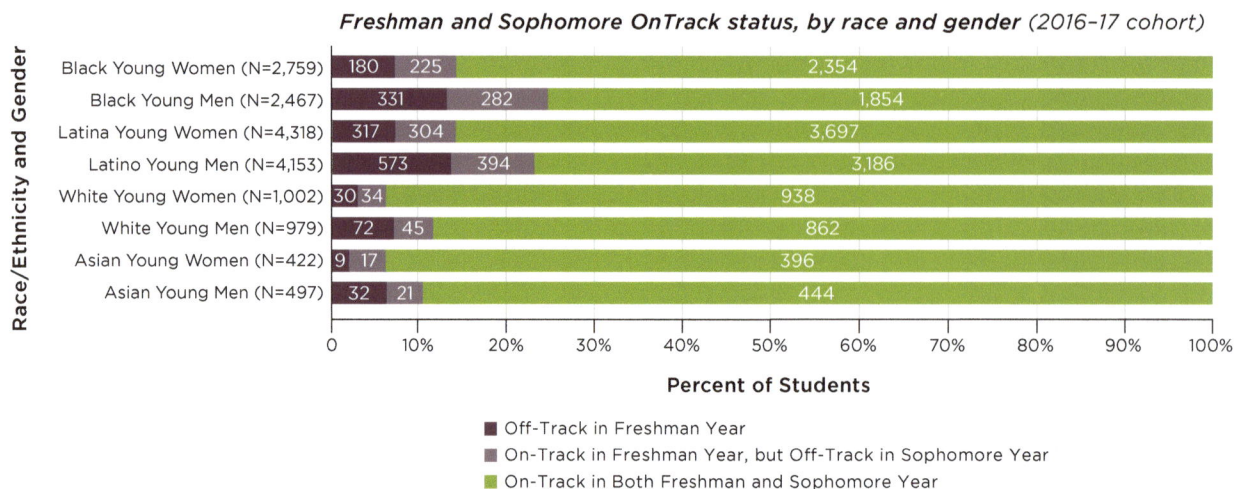

- ■ Off-Track in Freshman Year
- ■ On-Track in Freshman Year, but Off-Track in Sophomore Year
- ■ On-Track in Both Freshman and Sophomore Year

Note: Only students who were freshmen at CPS are included in sophomore analysis. Charter students are also excluded. For more information, see Appendix A.

TABLE 2

Graduation Rates by Freshman and Sophomore OnTrack Status (2014–15 Cohort)

Freshman OnTrack Status		Sophomore OnTrack Status		Graduation Rate
On-Track	+	On-Track	→	**93%** (N=13,819)
Off-Track	+	On-Track	→	**73%** (N=487)
On-Track	+	Off-Track	→	**43%** (N=1,301)
Off-Track	+	Off-Track	→	**21%** (N=1,647)

Note: Only students whose CPS freshman and sophomore grades and attendance data were available are included. Charter students are excluded for this reason. Graduation status is based on whether a student graduated from CPS within four years of starting high school. For more information, see Appendix A.

Both freshman and sophomore performance are also important for students' likelihood of enrolling in a four-year college (**see Figure 20**).

However, sophomore year also presents an opportunity for some students who struggled as freshmen to get back on-track to high school graduation and college enrollment. Among Off-Track and On-Track Warning freshmen, the roughly 1,000 students who were able to earn a status of On-Track Below 3.0 or On-Track Above 3.0 in sophomore year graduated at rates comparable to those of their peers who had been on-track as freshmen (**see Figure 19**). Freshman year remains the most critical, but schools have an opportunity to further boost their students' high school graduation rates and college success by providing support to struggling sophomores, as well.

FIGURE 19

Freshman and Sophomore Success Both Matter for High School Graduation

High school graduation rates, by Freshman and Sophomore Success Categories *(2014–15 cohort)*

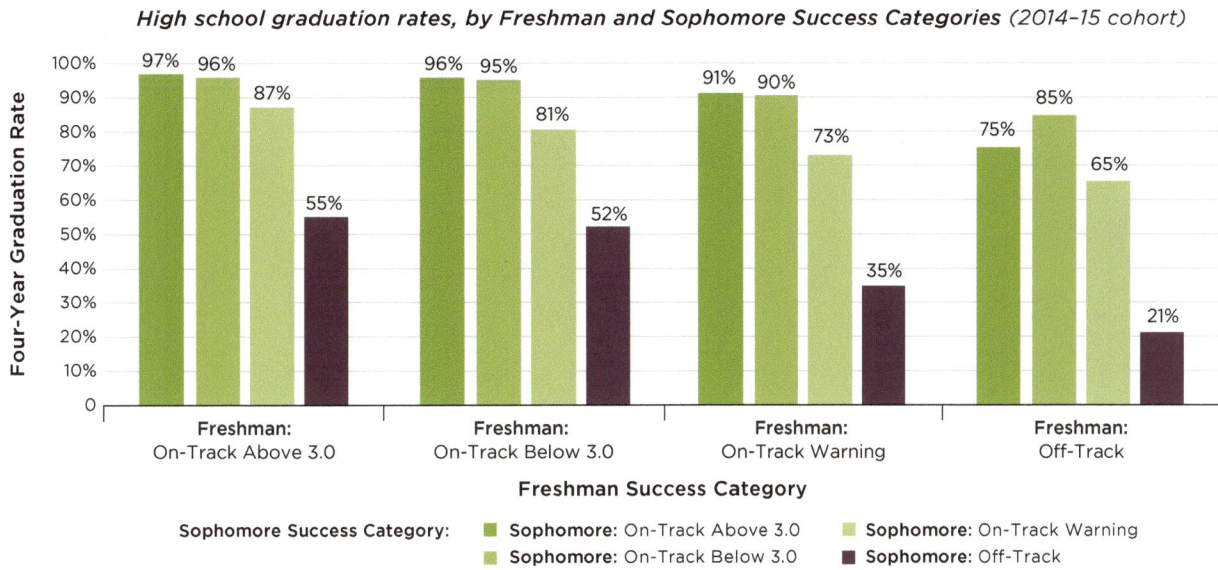

Note: Only students who were freshmen at CPS are included in sophomore analysis. Charter students are also excluded. Graduation status is based on whether a student graduated from CPS within four years of starting high school. For more information, see Appendix A.

FIGURE 20

Students Who Earned a GPA of 3.0 or Higher as Freshmen and Sophomores Were Most Likely to Enroll Immediately in a Four-Year College

Immediate four-year college enrollment rates, by Freshman and Sophomore Success Categories *(2014–15 cohort)*

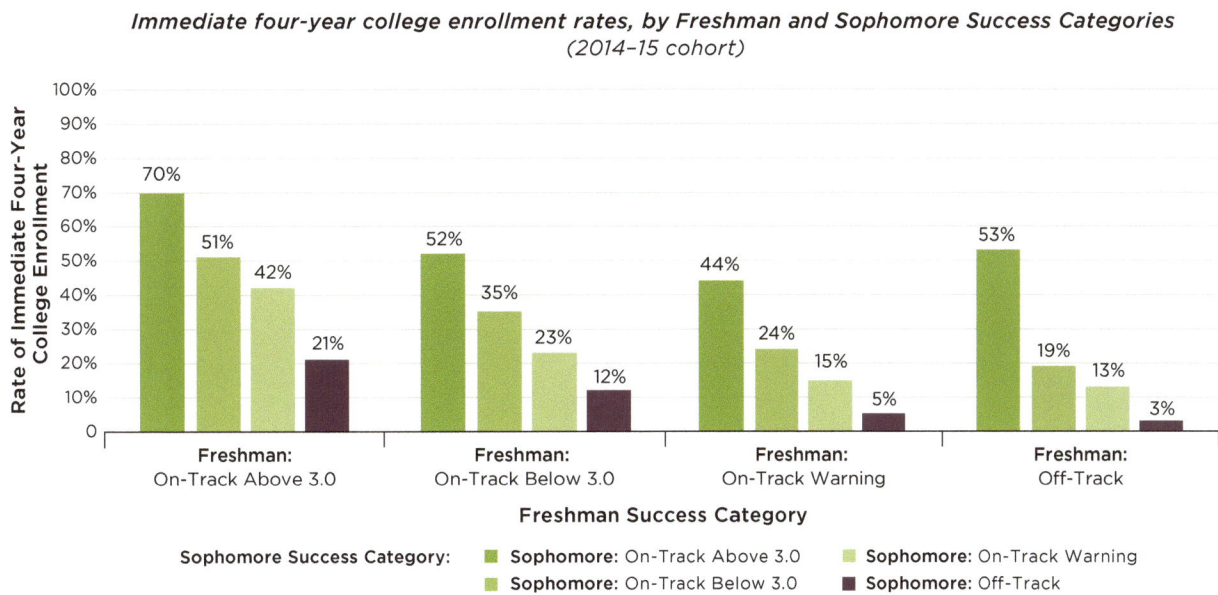

Note: Only students who were freshmen at CPS are included in sophomore analysis. Charter students are also excluded. Immediate four-year college enrollment status is based on whether students graduated within four years of starting high school, then enrolled in a four-year college in the fall following their high school graduation. For more information, see Appendix A.

CHAPTER 6

Interpretive Summary

Sophomore year is a time of tremendous opportunity for high school students in Chicago. Using Freshman OnTrack and more nuanced Freshman Success Categories, sophomore educators can better target intervention and support from the beginning of sophomore year. Using Sophomore OnTrack and Sophomore Success Categories, they can monitor and support students during sophomore year.

This study offers six key points for consideration:

1. **Sophomore year presents educators with an additional opportunity to identify and intervene with students who need more support.** At the beginning of sophomore year, with some relatively simple indicators—freshman off-track status, low attendance, and course failures—sophomore educators can identify about 70 percent of the students who are unlikely to graduate without additional intervention. By the end of sophomore year, this percentage can be as high as 85 percent. By layering on GPA, educators can further identify students who need additional support to gain access to selective post-secondary opportunities. Importantly, these percentages are not determinative: instead, they suggest that monitoring and increased support for sophomores could lead to more students graduating from high school and enrolling in college.

2. **For students who were off-track during freshman year, sophomore year can be an opportunity to recover. For some students who were on-track during freshman year, especially those with any Fs or low attendance, sophomore year is a critical year on the path to high school graduation.** There can be meaningful movement in students' performance from freshman to sophomore year, and movement between Success Categories can have significant implications for students' eventual outcomes.

Though it is relatively uncommon, students who finished freshman year off-track but got back on-track sophomore year graduated at a rate similar to the district's overall high school graduation rate. On the other hand, of the students who were off-track sophomore year, nearly one-half had been on-track as freshmen, and very few of these students went on to graduate within four years. This movement between Success Categories highlights that, like freshman year, sophomore year holds both opportunity and risk, and a responsibility for educators.

3. **Freshman year remains the most critical year in students' educational trajectories, and even with rising Freshman OnTrack rates, the Freshman OnTrack metric remains predictive of high school graduation.** The findings from this report confirm previous findings from the UChicago Consortium and others about the importance of freshman year. Nearly 50 percent of non-graduates were off-track during freshman year, and another 20 percent showed an additional warning indicator—a low attendance rate or a course failure—during their freshman year. We don't have to wait until sophomore year to use accurate indicators: with careful monitoring of data, freshman educators can identify most students in danger of not graduating and provide support to help them succeed.

4. **Educators can monitor more subtle warning indicators, including low attendance rates and all course failures, to provide support to a wider group of students in need.** The Freshman OnTrack indicator has remained a stable predictor of students' likelihood of graduation, and monitoring of Sophomore OnTrack has become more widespread across CPS. The next step is for schools to use more nuanced indicators to identify students who are likely to need further support in order to be successful. For a district that now has Freshman and Sophomore OnTrack Rates at 85 percent or higher, it may make sense to begin considering adopting additional indicators.

5. **Freshmen and sophomores with strong grades but low attendance are in danger of not graduating, and need additional monitoring and support.** Freshman and sophomore attendance can provide insight into students' likelihood of graduating from high school, independent of their freshman grades and course failures. Students with attendance rates below 85 percent during their freshman year were just as likely to not graduate as students who were off-track, and even students who passed their courses with high grades were in danger of not graduating from high school if they missed three or more days per month. Incorporating indicators based on attendance can help educators identify and intervene earlier with more of these students.

6. **Applying these findings to sophomore year will require intentional shifts and work on the part of central office, networks, and schools.** The Freshman OnTrack indicator only took root when schools made changes to systems and structures in order to effectively and efficiently use data. In order to replicate some of the success of Freshman OnTrack in sophomore year, the district will have to devote the resources necessary to expand the work of disaggregating freshman and sophomore year indicators, and to intentionally bring sophomore educators into teams with training to analyze student data and co-plan interventions together. Fortunately, the district and its schools don't have to reinvent the wheel; they can learn from the work already done around Freshman OnTrack and freshman success. Expanding this work to sophomore year could have a significant impact on students.

References

Allensworth, E.M., & Clark, K. (2018)
Are GPAs an inconsistent measure of college readiness across high schools? Examining assumptions about grades versus standardized test scores (Working Paper). Chicago, IL: University of Chicago Consortium on School Research.

Allensworth, E., & Easton, J.Q. (2005)
The on-track indicator as a predictor of high school graduation. Chicago, IL: University of Chicago Consortium on Chicago School Research.

Allensworth, E., & Easton, J.Q. (2007)
What matters for staying on-track and graduating in Chicago Public Schools. Chicago, IL: University of Chicago Consortium on Chicago School Research.

Allensworth, E.M., Gwynne, J.A., Moore, P., & de la Torre, M. (2014)
Looking forward to high school and college: Middle grades indicators of readiness in Chicago Public Schools. Chicago, IL: University of Chicago Consortium on Chicago School Research.

Allensworth, E.M., Healey, K., Gwynne, J.A., & Crespin, R. (2016)
High school graduation rates through two decades of district change: The influence of policies, data records, and demographic shifts. Chicago, IL: University of Chicago Consortium on Chicago School Research

Allensworth, E.M., Nagaoka, J., & Johnson, D.W. (2018)
High school graduation and college readiness indicator systems: What we know, what we need to know. Chicago, IL: University of Chicago Consortium on School Research.

Easton, J.Q., Johnson, E., & Sartain, L. (2017)
The predictive power of ninth-grade GPA. Chicago, IL: University of Chicago Consortium on School Research.

Phillips, E.K. (2019)
The make-or-break year: Solving the dropout crisis one ninth grader at a time. New York, NY: The New Press.

Roderick, M., Kelley-Kemple, T., Johnson, D.W., & Beechum, N.O. (2014)
Preventable failure: Improvements in long-term outcomes when high schools focused on the ninth grade year: Research summary. Chicago, IL: University of Chicago Consortium on Chicago School Research.

Roderick, M., Nagaoka, J., Allensworth, E., Coca, V., Correa, M., & Stoker, G. (2006)
From high school to the future: A first look at Chicago Public Schools graduates' college enrollment, college preparation, and graduation from four-year colleges. Chicago, IL: University of Chicago Consortium on Chicago School Research.

Appendix A
Data Definitions

For the purposes of this analysis, the freshman cohort for a given year is defined as the students who were enrolled in the ninth grade at a CPS high school for the first time during the school year. For example, the 2016–17 freshman cohort consists of the students who were ninth-graders at CPS for the first time during that school year.

Students were included in the sophomore analysis only if they were a member of a CPS freshman cohort. Their sophomore outcomes were defined as the outcomes from the year after their freshman year—typically tenth grade, though it was ninth grade for students who spent a second year in ninth grade. While the UChicago Consortium typically uses the terms "ninth grade" and "tenth grade", we chose to use the terms "freshman" and "sophomore" for this report given how we structured this sophomore analysis.

Because of limited data availability from charter schools, students who were enrolled at a CPS charter school during their first-time freshman year were excluded freshman analysis, and students who were enrolled at a CPS charter school during either freshman or sophomore year were excluded from sophomore analysis. Students marked as having left CPS during freshman or sophomore year for a reason other than dropping out of high school, including transfer to another school district, were excluded from the analysis.

Graduation rates are calculated based on students' outcomes four years after their first-time freshman year of high school. Diplomas from Options Schools were not counted toward graduation rates. Immediate college enrollment is defined as enrolling in a college during the fall term immediately following students' graduation from CPS. Students marked as having left CPS within four years of high school for a reason other than dropping out of high school, including transfer to another school district, were not included in the denominator of graduation or college enrollment rates.

GPAs are a weighted average of students' course grades. They are weighted by number of credits, but not by course level. Students' attendance rate for a given school year was calculated as the total number of days attended during the school year divided by the total number of days enrolled during the school year.

Appendix B

Freshman OnTrack and High School Graduation Rates Over Time at CPS

Freshman OnTrack and graduation rates at CPS have grown significantly over the past decade.

FIGURE B.1

After CPS Schools Began Receiving Regular Freshman OnTrack Data in 2008, the Growth in the Freshman OnTrack Rate Accelerated

Freshman OnTrack rates of CPS freshman cohorts

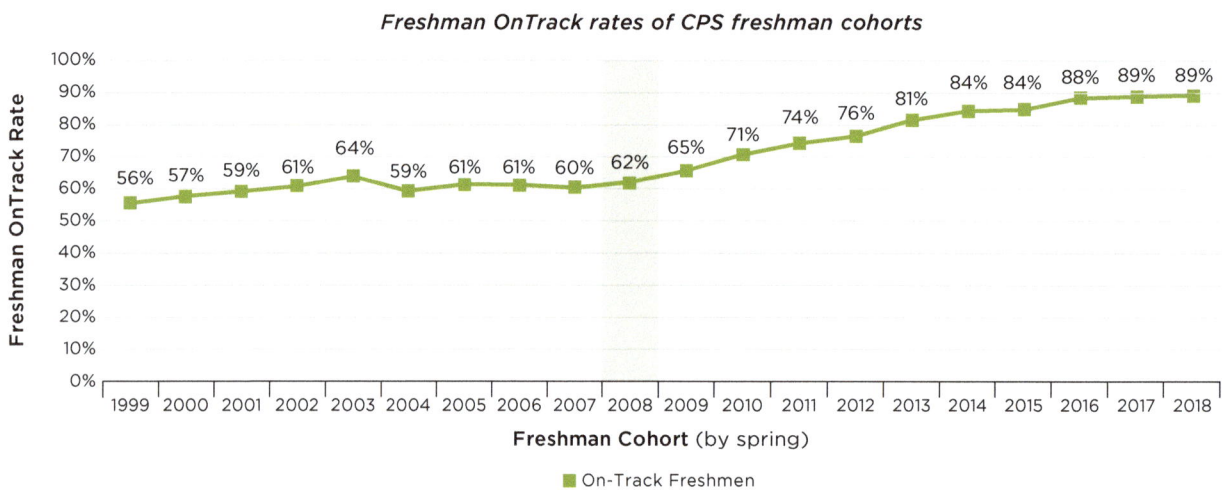

Freshman Cohort (by spring)

■ On-Track Freshmen

Note: Freshman cohorts are labelled based on the spring of students' first-time freshman year at CPS. Charter students are excluded from this analysis. For more information, see Appendix A.

FIGURE B.2

As the Freshman OnTrack Rate Has Increased, the High School Graduation Rate has Increased for the Same Cohorts of Students

Graduation rates of CPS freshman cohorts

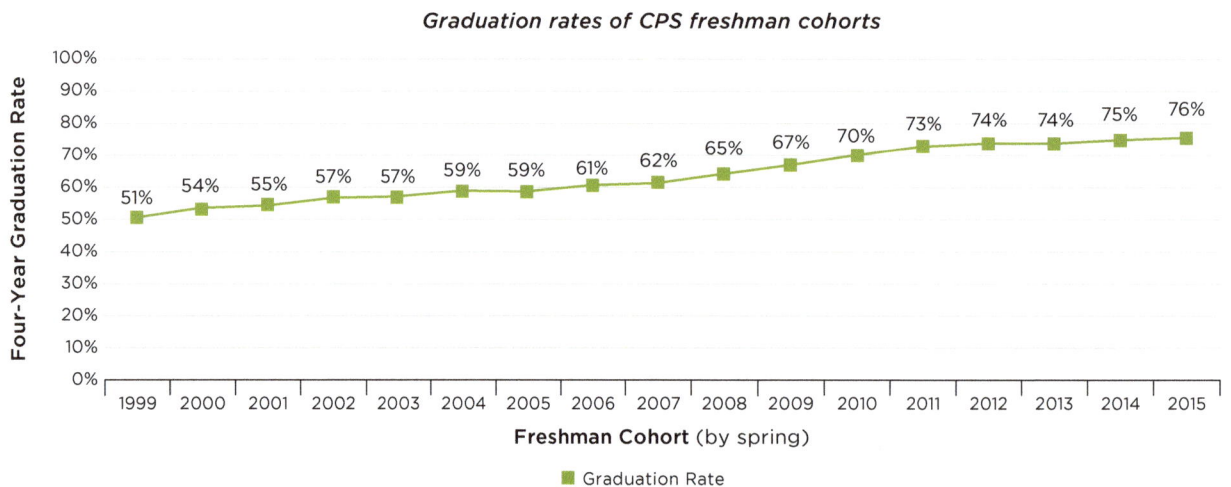

Freshman Cohort (by spring)

■ Graduation Rate

Note: Freshman cohorts are labelled based on the spring of students' first-time freshman year at CPS. Graduation status is based on whether a student graduated from CPS within four years of starting high school. For more information, see Appendix A.

FIGURE B.3

The Graduation Rate Has Increased for Students of All Races and Genders, though Overall Disparities in Outcomes Remain

Growth in CPS graduation rates over time, by race/ethnicity and gender

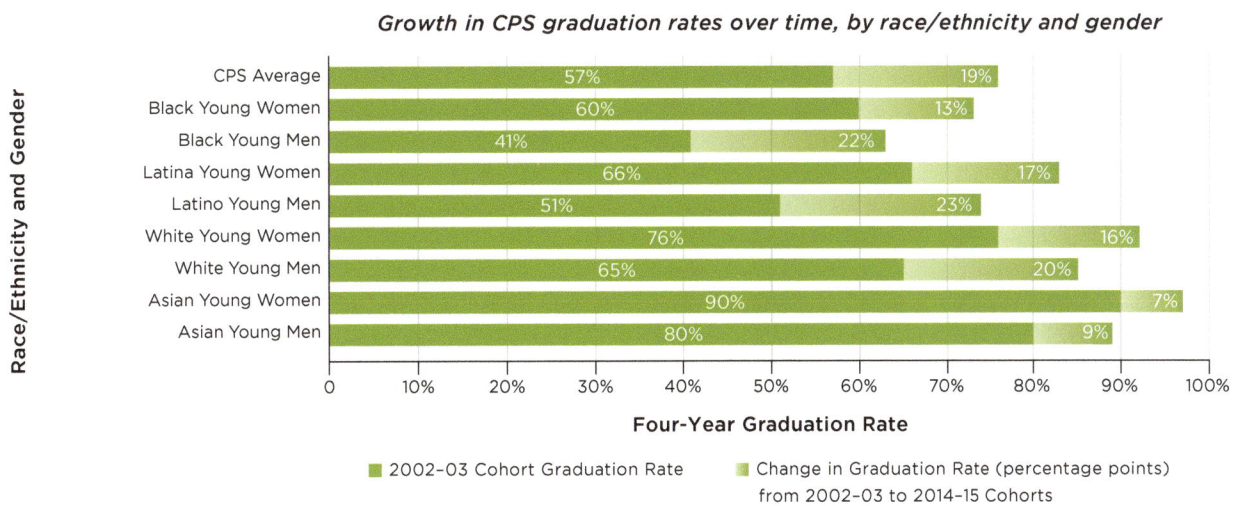

Four-Year Graduation Rate

■ 2002–03 Cohort Graduation Rate   ▣ Change in Graduation Rate (percentage points) from 2002–03 to 2014–15 Cohorts

Note: Graduation status is based on whether a student graduated from CPS within four years of starting high school. This figure shows the difference between the graduation rates of the 2002-03 freshman cohort and the 2014-15 freshman cohort, by race/ethnicity and gender. For example, the four-year high school graduation rate for the Latina young women from the 2002-03 cohort was 66 percent. Twelve years later, the graduation rate for the Latina young women from the 2014-15 cohort

Appendix C

Relationships between Freshman and Sophomore Course Failures and High School Graduation

Course failures during the first two years of high school are highly predictive of non-graduation. Every additional failure during freshman or sophomore year indicates a decreased likelihood of graduating from high school.

FIGURE C.1

Freshman Course Failures Are Predictive of Non-Graduation

Graduation rate, by number of freshman course failures (2014–15 cohort)

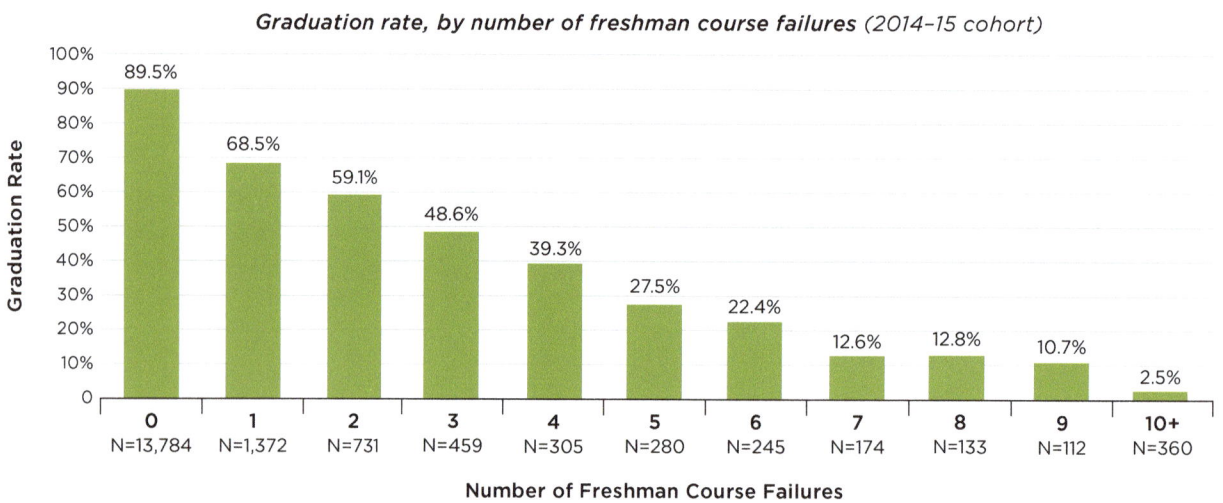

Number of Freshman Course Failures	Graduation Rate
0 (N=13,784)	89.5%
1 (N=1,372)	68.5%
2 (N=731)	59.1%
3 (N=459)	48.6%
4 (N=305)	39.3%
5 (N=280)	27.5%
6 (N=245)	22.4%
7 (N=174)	12.6%
8 (N=133)	12.8%
9 (N=112)	10.7%
10+ (N=360)	2.5%

Note: Charter students are excluded from this analysis. Graduation status is based on whether a student graduated from CPS within four years of starting high school. For more information, see Appendix A.

FIGURE C.2

Sophomore Course Failures Are Predictive of Non-Graduation

Graduation rate, by number of sophomore course failures (2014–15 cohort)

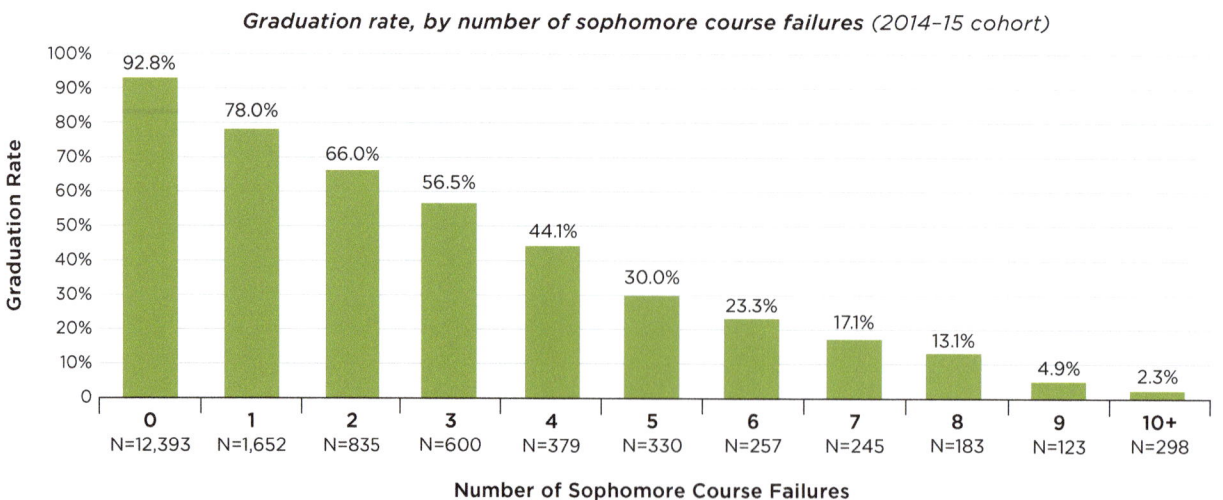

Number of Sophomore Course Failures	Graduation Rate
0 (N=12,393)	92.8%
1 (N=1,652)	78.0%
2 (N=835)	66.0%
3 (N=600)	56.5%
4 (N=379)	44.1%
5 (N=330)	30.0%
6 (N=257)	23.3%
7 (N=245)	17.1%
8 (N=183)	13.1%
9 (N=123)	4.9%
10+ (N=298)	2.3%

Note: Only students who were freshmen at CPS are included in sophomore analysis. Graduation status is based on whether a student graduated from CPS within four years of starting high school. Charter students are also excluded. For more information, see Appendix A.

Appendix D

Predictivity of Freshman and Sophomore Indicators of Graduation

These figures compare the sensitivities and false positive rates of several indicators of non-graduation. For freshmen, an overall GPA below 1.5 and an attendance rate below 85 percent each have a similar sensitivity and false positive rate to an off-track status, while a failure in any course and an attendance rate less than 90 percent each have a higher sensitivity and a higher false positive rate.

FIGURE D.1

Sensitivity and False Positive Rates of Freshman Indicators of High School Graduation

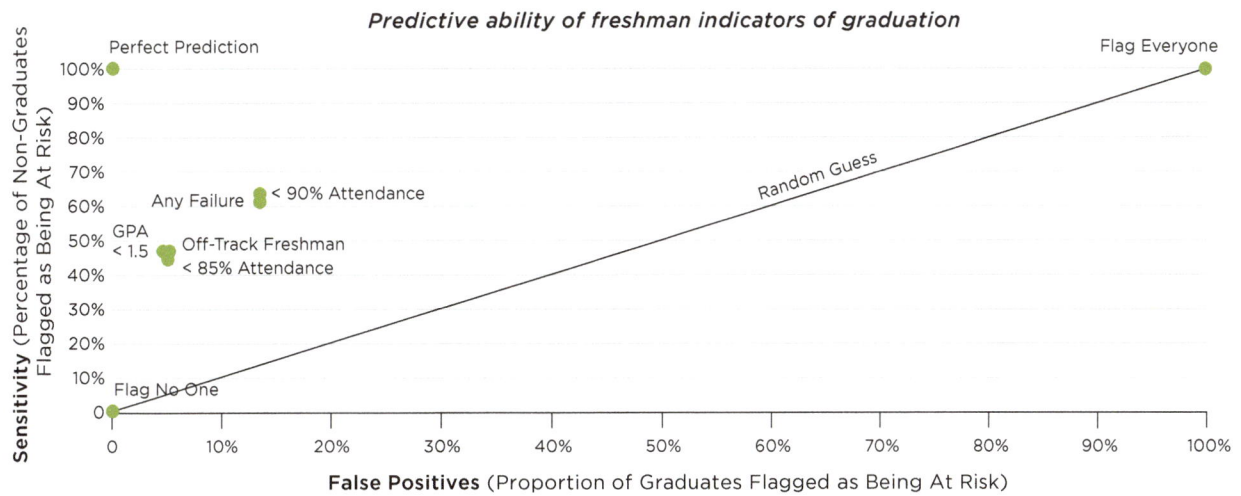

Predictive ability of freshman indicators of graduation

Note: Sensitivity and false positive rate are calculated using outcomes of 2014–15 freshmen. Charter students are excluded from this analysis. Graduation status is based on whether a student graduated from CPS within four years of starting high school. For more information, see Appendix A.

FIGURE D.2

Sensitivity and False Positive Rates of Sophomore Indicators of Graduation

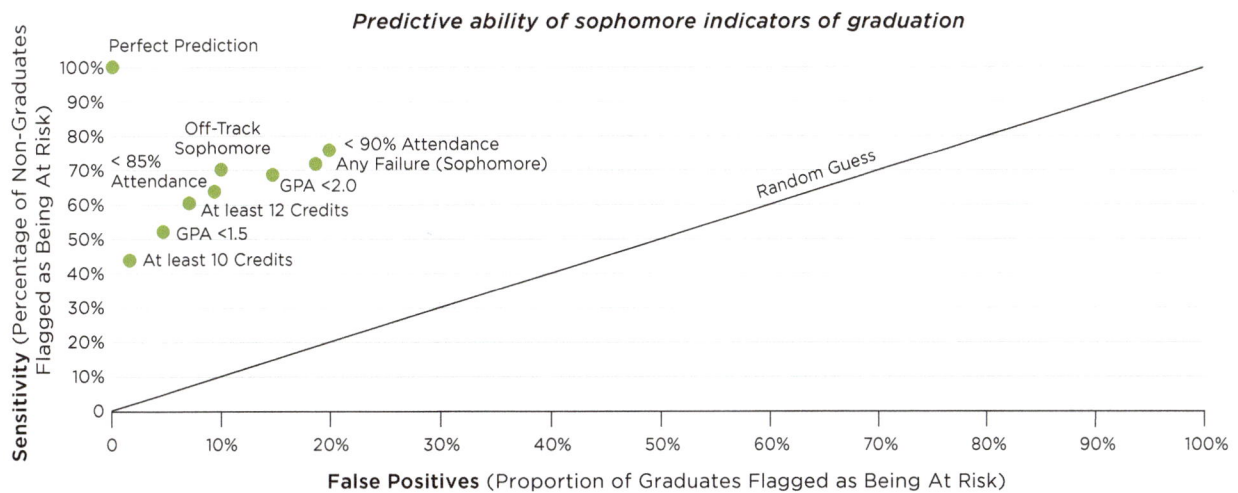

Predictive ability of sophomore indicators of graduation

Note: Sensitivity and false positive rate are calculated using outcomes of 2014–15 freshmen. Only students who were freshmen at CPS are included in sophomore analysis. Charter students are also excluded. Graduation status is based on whether a student graduated from CPS within four years of starting high school. For more information, see Appendix A.

ABOUT THE AUTHORS

ALEX SEESKIN is the Director of the To&Through Project. Prior to coming to To&Through, Alex taught high school English in CPS for seven years, serving as the English Department Chair at Lake View High School from 2008–12. He earned a BS in communications from Northwestern University and an EdLD from the Harvard Graduate School of Education.

SHELBY MAHAFFIE is a Research Analyst at the UChicago Consortium and the To&Through Project. Prior to joining the Consortium and To&Through, she worked as a research assistant at the University of Chicago Urban Labs. Shelby received her BA in economics and public policy from the University of Chicago.

ALEXANDRA USHER is an Associate Director of the To&Through Project and a Senior Research Analyst at the UChicago Consortium, where she leads the research and data processes that inform the To&Through Project. Alexandra most recently led data strategy for the AUSL network of schools, and prior to that spent time at CPS and the Center on Education Policy. She holds a BA in international affairs from the George Washington University and an MPP from the University of Chicago Harris School.

The To&Through Project In collaboration with educators, policymakers, and communities, the To&Through Project aims to significantly increase high school and postsecondary completion for under-resourced students of color in Chicago and around the country by providing education stakeholders with research-based data on students' educational experiences and facilitating dialogue on its implications for adult practice. At the To&Through Project, we:

- Conduct research and publish data on what matters for the attainment of Chicago Public Schools students (in collaboration with the University of Chicago Consortium on School Research).
- Design data tools and resources for education stakeholders that make data meaningful and actionable, including the publicly available To&Through Online Tool.

- Foster conversations about what matters most for students' high school and post-secondary success.
- Facilitate a network of middle grades educators committed to building more equitable and supportive educational environments that promote the success of middle grades students in high school and beyond.

The To&Through Project is located at the University of Chicago's Urban Education Institute in the School of Social Service Administration.

Steering Committee

RAQUEL FARMER-HINTON
Co-Chair
University of Wisconsin, Milwaukee

JOHN ZIEGLER
Co-Chair
DePaul University

Institutional Members

SARAH DICKSON
Chicago Public Schools

BRENDA DIXON
Illinois State Board of Education

BOGDANA CHKOUMBOVA
Chicago Public Schools

TROY LARAVIERE
Chicago Principals and
Administrators Association

JESSE SHARKEY
Chicago Teachers Union

MAURICE SWINNEY
Chicago Public Schools

Individual Members

NANCY CHAVEZ
OneGoal

JAHMAL COLE
My Block, My Hood, My City

VERNEE GREEN
Mikva Challenge

MEGAN HOUGARD
Chicago Public Schools

GREG JONES
The Academy Group

PRANAV KOTHARI
Revolution Impact, LLC

AMANDA LEWIS
University of Illinois at Chicago

RITO MARTINEZ
Surge Institute

SHAZIA MILLER
NORC at the University of Chicago

CRISTINA PACIONE-ZAYAS
Erikson Institute

KAFI MORAGNE-PATTERSON
UChicago Office of Civic
Engagement

LES PLEWA
William H. Taft High School

PAIGE PONDER
One Million Degrees

ELLEN SCHUMER
COFI

REBECCA VONDERLACK-NAVARRO
Latino Policy Forum

PAM WITMER
Office of the Mayor, City of Chicago

www.ingramcontent.com/pod-product-compliance
Lightning Source LLC
Chambersburg PA
CBHW041429090426
42741CB00003B/98